Advance Praise for
Gifts from the Broken Jar

"In this extraordinary and beautifully written memoir, PJ Long shows us that the soul is different from the brain, and that the cracks in our physical being are the places where the light comes through. *Gifts from the Broken Jar* is a book for anyone seeking that authentic wholeness which is our common birthright, the shining gold coin of which our deepest humanity is made." ~ **Rachel Naomi Remen, M.D., author,** *Kitchen Table Wisdom* **and** *My Grandfather's Blessings*

"Awesome. I was often struck by how beautifully PJ wove her experience into words. She has written a book that will help or inspire those who are navigating their own darkness." ~ **Sherry Strafford Rediger, Ph.D., Marriage and Family Therapist**

"This deceptively simple book holds you in its words as if in a best friend's arms. . . . It encourages you to risk reaching out to a wounded aspect of yourself and give her refuge. It reminds you that life will bring pain, but it is within each of us to heal our own hearts. PJ's mother taught her that we don't pay back the good things that happen to us, we just pass them along. This book is a very good thing that will happen to all who read it." ~ **Dawna Markova, Ph.D, author,** *I Will Not Die an Unlived Life;* **co-editor,** *Random Acts of Kindness* **and** *Kids' Random Acts of Kindness*

"Some of the most beautiful prose I have ever had the privilege of reading. I will be the first in line to buy copies." ~ **Anne McManus, former Executive Director, HOPE Adoptions and Family Services International**

"PJ is a wise and loving person whose journey touches our deepest core. I found myself carrying *Gifts from the Broken Jar* with me to remain connected to PJ's patience, grace, and immense courage. Silent tears kept coming as I felt her pain, her joy, her strength. . . . Not only do we learn about traumatic brain injury and rehab, but we learn how to be a close friend, spouse, mother. We learn how to fill ourselves with patience, grace, humor, and love. We learn how to be." ~ **Jackie Waldman, author,** *The Courage to Give* **series**

"Ms. Long has exquisitely crafted a book that can help people understand the many ramifications of brain injury. . . . She has portrayed a realistic recovery with the compensations that make daily life workable."
~ **Roxane Dean, ACSW, LCSW, Information and Resource Manager, Brain Injury Association of America**

"*Gifts from the Broken Jar* is a powerful memoir that offers us invaluable insight into the process of healing and repair. Whenever our lives break we have to discover how to fit the pieces back together again. . . . PJ Long reminds us that we can carefully collect the broken shards and turn them into a thing of beauty, a mosaic for all to behold." ~ **Naomi Levy, author, *To Begin Again: The Journey Toward Comfort, Strength, and Faith in Difficult Times***

"PJ has put into words exactly what I'm feeling but can't explain. I feel that I've found a soulmate in the pages of the book." ~ **A brain cancer patient**

"PJ Long's journal is certainly a record of a resilient spirit struggling back to self-reliance, but it is also an homage to the power of the word. Here we see a woman learning to put sentences together again, and in the process, finding the self that nests in language. As a writer, I was reminded of how powerful our voices are, each and every one. . . . *Gifts from the Broken Jar* is courageous and joyful and a pleasure to read." ~ **Sandra Scofield, author, *Occasions of Sin: A Memoir***

"I love this book! It's filled with so much beauty and wisdom, inspiration and hope. PJ's insights are such a gift!" ~ **M.J.B., homeschooling mother of three**

"Inspiring and unique. . . . PJ's interactions and struggles as a mother, wife, and friend are profound and thought-provoking. A must-read message for professionals, individuals with traumatic brain injury, and their families to instill acceptance, but most importantly, hope." ~ **Lorraine Wargo, TBI Program Coordinator, Division of Vocational Rehabilitation, State of Vermont**

"*Gifts from the Broken Jar* is a lovely piece of contemplative writing, rich in imagery and insight." ~ **Cheri Register, author, *The Chronic Illness Experience: Embracing the Imperfect Life***

"The terrible isolation and mental chaos caused by brain injury is a metaphor for each of us who struggles through the multiple losses of illness. In the prayerfulness of elegant writing, we are invited into the beauty of place, the wisdom of children, the constancy of a spouse, the loving kindness of a parent, the blessings of animals, as PJ courageously tries to inventory and order the world around her . . . . PJ's book makes us wonder, along with her, if what we think of as 'self' actually isn't." ~ **The Reverend Maggie Rebmann, The Unitarian Church of Montpelier, Vermont**

"PJ's story is very personal, yet universal, as are the healing and the mending and the self-realizations. There are so many gems that the reader can hold, mull over, and carry away. It's a beautiful, beautiful book." ~ **Jerri Andersen, mother and widow, New York City**

"PJ Long has done a real service by writing this book. I enthusiastically recommend it for all brain injury survivors and family members." ~ **Jim Vyhnak, Executive Director, Brain Injury Association of Vermont and TBI survivor**

"I read the first thirty pages without even sitting down. PJ Long truly has a gift for writing." ~ **Mary Marlow, The Book Mouse Bookshop, Atkinson, NH**

Gifts

from the

Broken

Jar

Rediscovering Hope, Beauty, and Joy

P J L O N G

EQUI
LIBRIUM
P R E S S

Books that inform and inspire

Foreword © 2005 by Christin Lore Weber

"On Eagle's Wings" by Michael Joncas ©1979, OCP Publications, 5536 NE Hassalo, Portland OR 97213. All rights reserved. Used with permission. "When Autumn Mists Gather" from *The Waldorf Song Book*, edited by Brien Masters. Reproduced with the permission of Floris Books, Edinburgh. "It Is Ours to Praise" Copyright © 1996 by Marcia Lee Falk. Excerpted from *The Book of Blessings: New Jewish Prayers for Daily Life, the Sabbath, and the New Moon Festival* by Marcia Falk (Harper, 1996; paperback edition, Beacon Press, 1999). Used by permission. Quotation from Chief Dhyani Ywahoo, used with her kind permission. Excerpts from *Altar Music* by Christin Lore Weber reprinted with permission from Scribner, an imprint of Simon & Schuster Adult Publishing Group. Copyright © 2000 by Christin Lore Weber.

Published by:

EquiLibrium Press, Inc.
10736 Jefferson Blvd. #680
Culver City, CA 90230 USA
www.equipress.com

EquiLibrium Press logo and "Books that inform and inspire" are registered trademarks of EquiLibrium Press, Inc.

Cover and interior design: Mayapriya Long, *www.bookwrights.com*

Printed in the United States of America

Publisher's Cataloging-in-Publication Data
(Prepared by The Donohue Group, Inc.)

Long, PJ (Patricia JoAnn), 1959-
  Gifts from the broken jar / PJ Long.
  p. ; cm.
  Includes bibliographical references.
  ISBN: 0-9667393-9-6

1. Long, PJ (Patricia JoAnn), 1959---Health. 2. Life change events--Psychological aspects. 3. Adjustment (Psychology) 4. Self-actualization (Psychology) 5. Brain damage--Patients--United States--Biography. I. Title.

BF637.L53 L66 2005
155.916

For

Benjamin and Ekta,
precious jewels of my heart,

and for

Michael,
who kept his promise.

Contents

Foreword *by Christin Lore Weber* • xi

Prologue • 2

Summer 2000— *Patience*

   1. Sour Milk • 16

   2. Pomegranates and Figs • 31

   3. Morning Glory • 42

Autumn 2000— *Faith*

   4. Climbing • 54

   5. Singing Up a Rainbow • 66

   6. Traffic Jam • 83

Winter 2001— *Acceptance*

   7. Snowed In • 102

   8. Moving Out • 113

Spring 2001— *Gratitude*

   9. Honeymoon • 128

   10. Seedlings • 143

Summer 2001— *Humility*

  11. Regeneration • 154

Autumn 2001— *Compassion*

  12. Terrible Days • 166

Winter 2002— *Hope*

  13. Bravery and Dreams • 176

Spring 2002— *Beauty*

  14. Peepers' Song • 188
  15. Cake and Lemonade • 198

Summer 2002— *Joy*

  16. Confidence • 210
  17. The Broken Jar • 225
  18. Shiny Shoes • 239

Notes and Acknowledgements • 250
About the Author • 253

Foreword

PJ always sent a Christmas gift. I have a whole collection of handmade Christmas angels that I lift from their tissue paper each year to decorate the tree or place in choice locations around the house. Once she sent a spirit doll made of memories: fabric scraps from her son's baby blanket, a lacy slip that had belonged to her grandmother, a piece of veil with golden stars PJ wore in a ritual dance she choreographed in my living room and performed as part of her masters thesis.

Besides her yearly gift, PJ wrote a Christmas letter that I anticipated reading because of her ability to weave stories from the small events of everyday life. Her children, Benjamin and Ekta, managed each year to say or do something simple but stunning from which PJ would draw inspiration and wisdom. The letter always ended with a note from her husband, Michael, and everyone's signature—even when the children's were only scribbles.

In 1999, no gift arrived. Though my own life that December felt caught in a whirlwind, I had done some Christmas shopping and sent PJ a necklace of tiny beads interspersed with petite dried roses. A local woman artist had made it, and I knew PJ would appreciate that the roses had been grown in the area close to my new home.

Sunlight slanted off the snow-capped mountains onto my dining room table and the pile of cards I'd just brought in from the mailbox. I sorted through them and saw that PJ's 1999 Christmas letter had arrived. *Good*, I thought. *PJ's letter.* I slid the opener under the crease in the envelope, unfolded the letter, and began to read. But PJ hadn't written the letter that year; Michael had.

"John!" I called to my husband after reading the story Michael told. "PJ's been hurt. I think she's been hurt really bad."

I first met PJ in the late 1970s when both of us worked at St. Joseph's Home for Children in Minneapolis, a residential treatment center for children with emotional and developmental problems. She'd moved to Minnesota to be near Michael (then her fiancé) while he completed medical school, and also to pursue her own degree in psychology and communications. She attended classes by day and worked the night shift at the Home. Since I worked during the day, we might not have met at all, except that she stayed overtime one morning to attend a workshop I was giving. We were drawn into friendship almost immediately by our similar questions and concerns, and by the way our ideas seemed to build upon one another. Our age difference presented no obstacle—I am nearly two decades older—because we recognized in each other whole worlds of experience to share.

PJ always seemed older than she actually was. I remember wondering how one so young could have had her experiences and thought her thoughts. I had spent nearly all of my life in Minnesota, working for the Catholic Church—first as a nun and then as an educator and a chaplain. Rooted as I was in one place, I had attempted to delve deep. She, by contrast, had ranged wide. She lived in Saudi Arabia as a child, attended boarding schools in Massachusetts and Connecticut, went off to college in England at Oxford, and devoted a year to relief work in Bangladesh. PJ's world, to me, felt universal.

Our friendship has endured well over twenty years. We've been there for each other in the simple and the profound events of life. I participated in PJ's wedding to Michael. She was with me when my first husband died, and added the beauty of liturgical dance to his funeral. I held Benjamin when he was an infant, newly arrived in this country from India. PJ was with me when John and I were married. Even though we now live a continent away from one another, there has been no distance in our love.

By 1999, though, our communication had become sparse. PJ has always been a woman who immerses herself in the life that surrounds her. Her work—both as a psychotherapist and as an adjunct professor at a Vermont college—her civic involvement, and especially her beloved children, both still in grade school, took enormous time and energy. In November of 1999, when her customary birthday card didn't arrive, I'd assumed it was simply late. I had no idea that PJ was lying in bed, struggling to emerge from a thick pall of mental confusion and disconnection.

In his Christmas letter, Michael sent comfort to PJ's friends, saying she needed rest, that she had difficulty talking, that she would be better. In a reversal from all previous letters, PJ had added a short paragraph at the bottom of the page. To my mind, though, her few words bore the weight of proof: She would be fine. Surely anyone who could still write would be just fine.

A few weeks after receiving the letter, I entered a frenzied period with the publication of my novel, *Altar Music*. I signed one of the first copies of my book and sent it to PJ.

I didn't realize she was completely unable to read it. Instead, I learned later, she set it on the stand beside her bed and gazed at the picture on the cover. Above it she had hung the delicate necklace of roses.

Everything I wrote to PJ over the next few months was absorbed into her silence. But finally one afternoon in June when I opened the mailbox I saw an envelope inscribed in her familiar handwriting. I tore it open and read it while I walked back up the hill towards the house.

> Christin dear, your gifts are so lovely . . . your cards, your words, your book, your love, thank you for keeping me close, carrying me in your heart, my old self and my new self. Sometimes, I feel like a robot (well-programmed by people who love me greatly, but still a robot), as I go through my day. This brain injury led to my sort of "disappearing" from my life—like I've gone away. I re-enter slowly as my mind accommodates to new strategies and devices that help me function. I struggle to find my self, feel like my self—a new and different self.

> I've thought about things that might help me and I'd like to ask if you might be willing to do something for me. It would involve having conversations with me—not over the phone, because I don't process that quickly and can't sustain energy focus that long—but in writing, like on the e-mail. Conversations might be helpful to me... conversations that could happen slowly, quietly, like on paper—not face to face where the processing is so fast, and there is nothing written (which is hard because my memory doesn't hold things reliably in a useable way). Maybe I'm asking you to be a sort of therapist through letters—only I don't actually want a therapist so much as a friend who knew me well and out of that knowing and loving, can ask me questions and talk with me about life now, as I try to understand how my brain is working and who I'm becoming.

The minute I finished reading the letter, I began reading it again. I dashed into the house and read it to John. "She sounds really good, don't you think?" I felt ecstatic, like yelling her name into the mountains to hear it echo back. She'd sent her e-mail address, and I went immediately to the computer room to write to her, to tell her that nothing could give me more joy than to be with her, retrieving her memory and her voice through writing. We could write as many letters as it took, for as long as it took, for a lifetime if need be. It would be my deep pleasure, my joy. I signed off and clicked "Send."

Nothing came back. No message. No word. Not that day, not that week. It was as though I'd never answered her letter, as though she'd never written it. At first I assumed that PJ's injury simply slowed her response time. Then I began to wonder if PJ remembered that she had asked for my help. I wrote another e-mail plying her with questions: "Is it easier for you if I write e-mails, or if I send cards and letters through the mail? If I send an e-mail, do you remember that the e-mail is there? If I sent a card, would it be easier? You could hold it in your hands, and it would be there on your desk or by your bed. Is it easier to speak and write than it is to listen and read?"

PJ had completely forgotten that she had contacted me. Then, confused over the first e-mail I'd sent, she had accidentally deleted it and forgot about it. But she responded to the second e-mail immediately. As I read her descriptions of her situation, I began to imagine that words, for her, had become like disappearing ink, clear at first, but then fading almost immediately, replaced by the next word or sentence. Even if she printed out my e-mails, or kept my handwritten cards in front of her, she would have difficulty relating my response to her inquiry unless they were right next to each other.

Still, e-mail could be perfect—so much better than letters sent through the mail. Not only could the communications be more immediate and less prone to loss, but I could parse them. I could reply to PJ's e-mail by separating each of her sentences and writing my response directly underneath. She'd be able to see all the words, hers and mine, at one glance. It would look like dialogue for a screenplay.

It worked! PJ wrote:

Dear Christin,

This brings me to tears, or brings tears to me . . . whatever you say. I'm crying. I used to cry often and easily after the accident, and not know why or understand my emotional response, unable to have enough consciousness about it to be able to explain it to myself (or anyone else). Right now my printer is delivering pages and pages of conversation with you. And I am processing it bit by bit, very tiny bits, and feeling so nourished by the words. The words are opening up doors in my mind and bringing back parts of me to myself. What a miracle. It makes sense to me. I'm able to follow, taking in only what I can handle and relaxing because it's all right here in my fingers and it won't disappear, vanish somewhere in the ether of my head before I can grasp it. The mind clearly does not live in the brain, yet without the brain working smoothly, the mind is somewhat unreachable.

So we wrote to each other. Sometimes we wrote several times a day. I noticed over the months how her thoughts became clearer, less repetitive, more the flowing syntax that I remembered from before her accident. Then she had an amazing ability to see and express complex psychological and philosophical connections in vivid historical narrative. Now PJ had only the present moment. But she seemed to possess, maybe as a result of her injury, an increased awareness of each moment's sensate detail, and her written words captured those details with simplicity and a kind of startling color.

Who would have thought that what began so falteringly through a few e-mails, could have developed into such an accomplishment as PJ has achieved? Her courage, her strength, the fullness of her spirit, all are present here as a gift.

Remember when Anne Morrow Lindbergh went to her island and brought back her *Gift from the Sea*? As I read PJ's completed manuscript, I am aware that she has done much the same thing. Her island is a different one: it is an island of the mind where she has walked each day, gathering words that might prompt her own healing. But what she gathered has the potential to heal more than her own life. By her experience of looking at her world in a new way, PJ gives each of us a new perspective as well. The perspective is one of grace. Her gift to us is a new way of knowing by touch as she bends to gather the shells and stones of each moment. What stories she tells! What wisdom she now brings back from the island of her mind to share with us all.

— Christin Lore Weber

Prologue

On September 16, 1999, Hurricane Floyd made landfall in North Carolina and began its destructive path up the eastern coast of the United States. The following day, Vermont was deluged with rain and violent winds. By midafternoon, the sky was ominously dark. The streetlights were already on when I collected my children, Ekta and Benjamin, from school and headed to the stable where my daughter and I took riding lessons.

At the barn, the horses were uneasy. The old roof leaked and parts of the indoor ring were muddy. Metal roof panels were lifting and banging in the wind, and the whole place had a spooky feel. I had already decided that Ekta wouldn't ride, but it didn't feel right to cancel both lessons at the last minute. Besides, our instructor said the horses had been turned out earlier with no problems.

In retrospect, I know I should have followed my instincts, but back then I was willing to overrule my intuition simply to avoid disappointing this naïve young woman. Apparently, it didn't occur to her that I was a middle-aged mother with humble ambitions in the horse world. I dreamt of owning a couple of gentle farm horses that Ekta and I could take walking on sunny days in autumn woods. Toward that end this lesson was pointless, even dangerous. Still, I went ahead.

Every time the wind rattled the rafters, the mare I was riding spooked a little, tossing her head and jerking wildly. My instructor called to me to keep control, saying I should learn to manage a horse in all kinds of weather. I can't remember what happened next very clearly, only that the horse bolted and I couldn't hold her. She was cantering fast, coming into a curve, when she slipped in the mud. I do recall that as she lurched I rose out of the saddle, loosening my left foot from the stirrup in the hope that I could push away from her and not come down beneath her massive bulk. Then we both were flying. I flipped over in the air, my legs lifting up, and landed on my head. I bounced on impact, then landed on my head again.

That's how it happened, the brain damage that left me a stranger to myself.

The immediate aftermath was fairly unremarkable. I lost consciousness just briefly, and at first it seemed that I was only shaken. With help, I managed to walk to the barn office. I telephoned the health clinic and asked for my husband, Michael, Dr. Sampson. I told him that I had fallen, that I was fine, and that he should try to get home early, with pizza. Then I drove home and sank into the bathtub. By the time he arrived, I was nauseous. My neck and back were so sore that I stayed in bed all weekend.

On Monday Michael brought me a neck brace, which helped a little. I even went to my school board meeting that afternoon. As chair of the interview committee, I was screening candidates for administrative positions. I wasn't sure that I was up to it, but my calendar was very busy and I knew the meetings would be difficult to reschedule. I struggled through the first interview, my head swimming, my body aching, and then went home and returned to bed.

Tuesday morning I wanted to try going to work. I was a psychotherapist in private practice and didn't want to cancel appointments with people who relied on me. Yet in the first two sessions it became clear that I should have stayed home. I couldn't pay attention; it seemed as if I weren't even there. I knew I should be making comments and asking questions, but I couldn't come up with anything to say. I cancelled the rest of my appointments and headed home.

On the way, I stopped for groceries. I wandered aimlessly, not knowing what to buy. Standing in the cereal section,

I couldn't remember if my family ate cereal. I couldn't figure out why I was at the store or remember how I'd gotten there. I held fast to the empty grocery cart, my life buoy in the sea of chaos that threatened to drown me.

I finally left without buying a thing, managed to drive home, and called Michael. "I think something is wrong with me," I said. "Something bad. But I don't know what." He was upset that I had gone to work and sounded worried. He came home and brought me back to the clinic, where I had a cursory neurological exam and a few X-rays. The diagnosis was "post-concussive syndrome," meaning that the blow to my head had caused a variety of symptoms that all would disappear shortly. The doctor advised me to take it easy and assured me that I would be fine in a few days.

But I wasn't. The days passed; my symptoms did not. When a CAT scan revealed no bleeding, stroke, or other serious condition, my doctors reconfirmed that my symptoms were a result of the concussion: The fall had caused my brain to swell. Healing might take longer than they originally had thought, but all would be well soon.

Because I had lost the ability to recognize, much less explain, what I was experiencing, no one—including me—was fully aware of my symptoms or the extent of the damage to my brain. I was disoriented and dizzy, with a terrible headache. I couldn't read; I couldn't even look up a number in the phone book. I had no memory. I could not recall the names of my clients so they could be notified that I was unavailable. When anyone spoke to me I had trouble understanding what they were talking about. I slept most of the time, and when I was awake I hardly spoke. My body was a shell with no "me" inside.

Early in October, several weeks after my accident, Ekta begged me to go to our community theatre's annual production of *The Sound of Music*. She insisted that it would cheer me up. Instead, it overwhelmed me. I had to cover my ears and close my eyes for most of the evening because the sensory overload—from both the car ride and the play—was excruciating.

During intermission, a teenage girl sat down beside me on the refreshments bench and introduced herself as the owner of the horse that had thrown me. She had heard about my accident and had come to say how sorry she was. She told me that the horse was only a temporary boarder at the stable. Her own barn had collapsed the previous year in a storm, and the horse had barely broken out in time to escape the cave-in. According to the teen, my instructor knew of this traumatic history but hadn't mentioned it during my lesson because she didn't want me to be uneasy about riding in the storm.

Another month passed. My mother, who is a nurse, had moved in with us to care for me and manage our household. She says that I was a ghost in my own home, an ethereal spirit walking through unfamiliar territory. Like a baby, I was unable to perceive depth or height and would walk right off a stair landing, not realizing that I had to step down. I often was oblivious to other important details in my physical surroundings. I didn't notice when my husband or son left the toilet seat up, and sat down right into the bowl. One time I saw the seat up and, not wanting to fall into that cold water again, carefully lowered both seat and lid before sitting down. Moments later, I was completely baffled by the warm, wet puddle beneath me.

Michael told friends, "She has adjusted to her new life with a grace that truly amazes me." The truth is, I didn't have many thoughts, so how could I worry? I was lonely and discouraged, but I didn't have the capacity to analyze my situation and so couldn't feel much concern. And still I was sleeping close to twenty hours a day.

In our annual Christmas letter Michael described my accident and how the situation had stretched our family: "She can't drive, cook, grocery shop, or do third grade homework. Fortunately her mom and dad have been a tremendous help, and we are blessed with a community of supportive friends. But the children have had to adjust to a life where Mom is not like she used to be, and the myriad tasks of family management have fallen to their father, whose inattention to detail is renowned."

And he wrote about one of our weekly walks in the Von Trapp meadows: "Conversation for PJ was difficult; discussing the various facets of our life was clearly impossible. We simply walked, slowly and silently. Then she tightened her grasp on my arm and pointed. Two oak leaves twisted and twirled, chasing each other like two frenetic hummingbirds, up, down, and around. Caught in the currents between bare-tree mountains, never stopping, they danced. Since her brain is unable to process the busy, 'big stuff' of life, we have renewed appreciation for these often-overlooked small moments."

January. My calendar now was as bare as the snow-covered field outside my bedroom. The doctor's most recent estimate was that my recovery might take up to three months. That time had passed and yet something was still very wrong. It was apparent that the diagnosis of post-concussive syndrome was incomplete, because as some of my symptoms began to abate I became increasingly aware that I had more serious limitations.

My friend Helen tells me that one day when she visited I was trying to sort family photographs to re-orient myself to my life. But I couldn't put the pictures in the right sequence; I didn't remember that baby pictures come before school-age pictures. Even worse, I didn't recognize the life recorded in the photos.

I recall my mother helping me to organize my home work space to make room for a new computer. I had not been at my desk since the accident, and as she helped me sort through the piles that had accumulated, a disturbing phenomenon occurred: I had no connection to anything I picked up. I knew that I was sitting in my office—but only because I was in my own house, with my mother, and my name was on all the papers. I think I recognized my handwriting. Even so, it felt as if I was going through the belongings of someone who had died, glimpsing her life through a paper trail. It was interesting and I liked her work, but I didn't recognize any of it. As I realized that, I also became anxious.

My doctor consulted a neurologist and told me I just needed to give it more time.

I remember an evening in February. It was snowing, and I had gone out to sit on the porch swing after burning my hand yet again while cooking dinner. It was so hard to get the sequence right—potholder first, *then* you pick up the pan. As if that wasn't enough, I had slammed my fingers in the door on the way out. I was crying when Michael drove in from work. I watched him cross the driveway until he was standing before me at the bottom of the front steps.

"I'm not myself anymore," I said. "I don't know who I am, but I'm not myself. And I really miss that other person. She wasn't perfect, but I liked her. Now she's gone."

"I miss her too," Michael said. His eyes filled with tears. Then he added, "But you're still you, and I love you." He went on. "I don't know all the reasons I married you, but it wasn't just for your mind, and I'm not going to leave you, or stop loving you because you've lost it."

In late winter, trying to resurrect a familiar activity, I began rehearsals for a children's play at church. It was a simple tale that I had read to my own children a hundred times. I even had written the script the previous summer, but now I couldn't hold the story together in my mind. I had thought I would be well in time to direct the play, yet I was still frail and wobbly on my feet. I received a lot of help, enough that we were able to produce a wonderful show. But once the performance ended, I could barely stand. It was as though my brain had used up all the energy it could muster to get through the play. As I rose out of my chair to receive a bouquet of flowers, I fell.

Afterwards, people congratulated me on the play and said how glad they were to have me back, the PJ they knew so well. Those words were like a noose around my neck, and I felt the dissonance deep inside. I didn't know where that PJ had gone, but I knew she wasn't back, not yet.

April would be the seventh month, past the magic six-month date when the doctors had assured me that I would be well again. Wanting to do normal family things, thinking that would be good for all of us, we had planned a driving trip to Washington, D.C. At a rest stop on the highway, I stayed with the children so I wouldn't get lost. As we were walking back to the van, they handed me their drinks, large fat cups of soda. I held them, one in each hand, while the children climbed into their seats and buckled. Then somebody asked for a snack from the cooler that was right in front of me. Reaching to open it, I let go of both cups. When they landed at my feet, dousing me in soda from the waist down, I was totally puzzled, unaware that I had caused the mishap.

Once we arrived in Washington, I was eager to explore the Smithsonian. We never anticipated how easily my sensory filters could become overwhelmed. Unable to find my way around a display or process verbal directions, I became lost in the Air and Space Museum. I didn't realize that I needed to ask for help so that Michael could find me. By the time he did, I was in a full-blown panic, useless and crying uncontrollably. Later, at the Museum of Natural History, I nearly became lost again, caught in a sea of people trying to view the Hope Diamond.

Elsewhere, we came upon Dorothy's glittering ruby slippers from the Land of Oz. How I longed to slip my feet into them, click the heels, and say, "Take me home!" All the way home, back to myself.

Although some of my symptoms did disappear, many persisted. Michael and I began to suspect more pervasive brain damage, the kind that does not fully manifest until several months after an injury. Hoping to gain a better understanding of my condition and prognosis, I went for an evaluation at the University of Vermont's outpatient rehabilitation center. It would be a relief to finally have my impairments named, and to feel that someone was going to help me.

I met with a neuropsychologist, Dr. Owen Drudge, who outlined the tests, interviews, and procedures that would take place over the following six weeks. He assured me that after what had happened to me, profound fatigue was normal. I gave him a list of my other symptoms:

- skewed spatial and depth perception

- headaches and dizziness
- sensory overload
- inability to read or do simple math
- limited focus and concentration
- time disorientation
- inability to sort, organize, or plan
- difficulty making decisions or expressing ideas
- persistent feelings of isolation and sadness about the "me" who is gone

In the first months after the accident, I lacked the ability to realize that anything was wrong. At least now, after so many months of recovery—all those anguished, disappointing months of waiting—I finally was beyond that point.

The evaluation revealed that I had suffered a traumatic brain injury. The medical report explained that "although the initial injury presented as being mild in severity, she has experienced limitations and a recovery course more consistent with a moderately severe injury." I learned that I should not expect much more healing—the remaining physical damage could be permanent. Instead, any significant progress would come from rehabilitation, adaptation, and accommodation. In other words, I would need to learn strategies and make changes in daily living that would help me overcome my limitations. The treatment center would provide that training. But it was a ninety-minute trip, and I still couldn't drive.

Just as I was wondering how I'd manage these logistics, my mother called to say that she planned to devote her summer to helping with my rehab. I don't know if she's telepathic or whether she simply trusts her maternal instincts, but my mother has always had a way of showing up just when we need her. One day I asked, "How will we ever repay you for your many kindnesses?" (That's how Ekta refers to her grandmother's helping ways—"many kindnesses.") My mother replied, "We don't pay back the good things that happen to us. We just pass them along."

I looked forward to the day I would be well enough to offer a small "kindness" to somebody else. For now, with recovery consuming all my energy, I wondered what good things I possibly could pass along, even to my own children. While eleven year-old Benjamin seemed to be taking my condition in stride, Ekta, two years younger, was troubled. One day she observed, "Things can change in a minute, can't they? Your life is one way and then all of a sudden it's not anymore." For months she had been asking, "When will you be like our real mama again?" Now in my daughter's yearning I recognized my own, and her question was breaking my heart. Without the resources for motherhood that I'd once had in abundance, I did not feel like a "real mama" anymore.

I wanted to pick up my children at school like I used to do after a day at my office. We would stop for groceries, then drive home and make cookies or dinner while sharing stories about the day or doing homework together. Now I could barely navigate my way around the kitchen safely. I needed complete silence in order to accomplish the simplest of tasks, like unloading the dishwasher or mixing orange juice from frozen concentrate. I was scared of the garbage disposal and refused to use it if there was any conversation or activity nearby, lest I become distracted and lose my fingers down the drain. I couldn't even sauté an onion without explicit written directions reminding me to peel it first, *before* chopping. Baking chocolate chip cookies was absolutely out of the question.

As Mothers Day approached I sent a note to our minister, Maggie. In previous years I had always lit a church candle for the women who are my children's birthmothers in India and for birthmothers around the globe who are unable to raise the babies they bring to life. I would not be in church this Mothers Day—the auditory stimulation exhausted me—so I asked Maggie to light the candle for birthmothers unable to keep their children, and for all mothers whose circumstances somehow prevent them from being a real mama. How I longed to offer my true self to my children once more.

In June, Dr. Drudge referred me to a language pathologist for cognitive therapy and retraining. I was skeptical, even disappointed, that after all the testing he thought I needed to learn how to talk. But I wasn't in a position to turn anything down.

Very soon into the therapy, Lakshmi, my speech pathologist, wanted me to start writing. In the first months after my accident I was able to make simple notes, but that was all. Even now, nearly a year later, I still couldn't manage a paragraph. Lakshmi made me really angry the day she reviewed the writing process with me. As she patiently explained the structure of a paragraph—something I had done many times with Benjamin—I nearly exploded with the desire to yell, "I know *how* to do this. I just can't *do* it!"

Like my son, I had trouble encoding impressions into language, and I lacked sufficient working memory to hold onto thoughts long enough to write them out. I would lose the words almost as soon as I had formed a phrase in my mind. Looking back, I realize that I was expecting to write the way I used to: fluently, just by picking up a pen. I don't think I was aware of all this as I did the first writing assignments. I only knew that writing was beyond my grasp. I didn't understand that I could—I had to—train my mind in a new approach. Nevertheless, with Lakshmi's direction and encouragement, I produced my first piece, a short paragraph about our family's animals. She wanted me to write something every day. She suggested four or five sentences on a topic, saying that the more I practiced, the easier it would become.

That was when I had the idea to ask my friend Christin for help. I thought it might work better if I was actually "talking" to somebody real, rather than to a blank page. Besides, there was so much that I was trying to come to grips with in understanding what had happened to me, and who I was. I thought it would be helpful to have an older and wiser, trusted, intimate soulmate for the journey. Christin and I had been friends for over twenty years. If anyone could help me spin this straw into gold, she would be the one.

She had sent me a copy of her newly-published novel in March with a card that said, "A friend is an angel we can see and touch."

I needed her and happily she was there.

Patience

1

Sour Milk

*Journal: York Beach, Maine
A Thursday in June 2000*

Michael builds great sandcastles.

How lucky I am to have him as my life partner. And Ekta at nine is gangly and gorgeous, in love with the ocean, with the sand, her dad, everything.

The beach is deserted. One other sandcastle is the only evidence of today's other visitors. I'm so glad to be here on this beach, where I meet my old self and there is an easy, relaxed familiarity. I have a few "brain injury moments," like putting money in the wrong parking meter and conking out for a major nap at the usual time, but mostly I can carry on as though this were our last year's trip to Maine. And yet it's not.

Everything has changed since September's accident. All of us become a little different from one year to the next; that's the outcome of living. But these jarring transitions, the ones that shouldn't happen, they change our lives and leave us strangers to ourselves.

Who am I, now that the person I used to be has gone away?

I used to think it's just a matter of time. I thought I would wait patiently and one day she would return. Now I know it's not going to happen that way.

I think of an eighty year-old woman looking at a portrait of herself as a young mother, knowing that she was that woman once and now she is another. Awareness like that happens gradually over time, over decades, while life changes naturally and letting go is balanced with the new things we embrace in the next phase of life. If we are lucky. If we have what we need, growing old.

With me, the change was so sudden, and my mind—the instrument I have always relied on to steer a course through upheaval—was the very thing that became undependable.

The beach is like an empty set with the constant sounds of wind, the cries of gulls, and the crash of waves. Ekta's bright yellow T-shirt streaks the gray of dusk as she skips and jumps in the surf. Michael puts the finishing touches on their sandcastle, then runs to meet her and keeps on running, plunging into frigid Atlantic water.

Two elderly women stop to admire the castle and to take pictures from several different angles. Soon the tide will come in and the castle will disappear, photos the only evidence that it ever existed. What will the old women say when they show their pictures?

Today I bought blueberry jam for Gretchen, my sweet young newly-married neighbor. When I brought her some last summer we talked about my children and the children she was planning to have, about gardens and frogs and sunsets.

Then I fell off the horse, and in October Gretchen's malignant brain tumor was diagnosed. She had her surgeries and the radiation, and when she lost her lovely hair we created some silk wraps for her head. I sewed little caps, copying an old Tibetan beanie from my cedar chest. We still talk about her primroses, my lilacs, and the goslings that are grown up now down in the swamp. We talk about her dog and my children, about the watercolor-painted skies. But everything is different now, more precious.

Journal: Soccer camp

I'm thoroughly exhausted after spending the day away from home with no down time, no nap. While the children were at soccer camp, I went to their school to help plan for the fundraising dinner. Helen had assigned me some logistical things like supplies, table set-up, flowers, and room decorations. But after one bad nightmare and twenty-four hours of anxiety, I realized there were far too many details for me to handle. I offered to do flowers and design the room instead. It's not a major problem if I forget to put roses in the arrangement, but forgetting the forks, glasses, and chairs might be a significant showstopper.

I met with the woman who was in charge of the menu. My conversation notebook gave me a sense of competence. I think questions through in advance, and carefully record them. Then I simply had to write down her responses, and I could work with the information later.

After a tiring day, I made a bad decision to stop at the grocery store to pick up bread crumbs for the scallops recipe that was on the menu for dinner. Armed with my store map, I knew exactly where to go, and with the children's help I managed to get in and out fairly well at that busy hour. But my mind was swimming and I was struggling against extreme fatigue. As I walked out of the store I was trying to focus on traffic and went right to my usual parking spot, the place I always park Monday morning when I shop. I climbed in the car and was fumbling with my key in the ignition when both children, aghast, hollered, "Mom, that's not our car!"

In an instant I saw somebody else's upholstery, their stuff on the seat, their bag of chips (the kind I'd never buy). I jumped out quickly, totally lost. Thankfully, no alarm had brought the police asking questions I could not answer. And fortunately my little ones were at my side with reassuring words, guiding me across the lot to the right car and then home where, once I was safely on the couch and had recovered my dignity, we all had a great laugh. A good lesson: even the most reliable and well-designed strategy isn't foolproof. It wasn't Monday morning but Tuesday evening, I hadn't parked in my usual spot because it wasn't available, and I was much too tired to have successfully done such an errand.

Journal: Third day of soccer camp

Oh dear! When I went to wake Ekta this morning she was hiding under her covers, tears streaming down her lovely cheeks.

"What is it, darling? What's wrong?" I asked her.

"She didn't come." The words came out between her sobs.

"Who didn't come, sweetheart?"

"The tooth fairy. She never came to get my tooth."

How could I have forgotten? Her tooth had been dangling by a thread for about three weeks now. She pulled it out last night. What could I say? Perhaps I'd tell her that the tooth fairy spent the night in jail because she was trying to drive somebody else's car out of the grocery store parking lot.

Instead I said, "Maybe she couldn't get in because your window was closed."

She pulled back her curtain and showed me the window was cracked open.

"I think it's Benjamin's fault," she said. "He was probably sleep-talking and scared her away."

"Maybe so," I said, and began thinking of a way to redeem the magic.

As she got out of bed and headed for the bathroom she asked, "Was Dad on call last night? Maybe he was on the phone and that scared her."

"Yes, I'll go check the message machine. Then we'll know."

As I headed downstairs to find some money and a place to leave it, she called after me. "Mom! I know what happened; Minnow's snoring frightened her." My mother, known to her grandchildren as Minnow, was staying with us. "You know she sounds like a growling bear, so the tooth fairy flew off before she had a chance to get my tooth."

Downstairs, I tucked the money into a seashell, scribbled a note, and left it by Ekta's cereal bowl, which my mother was filling with oatmeal when, moments later, Ekta appeared.

That night at dinner she told Michael very excitedly about the extra money and the note. He explained how lucky it is to have a tooth that's not picked up. "It's like finding a four-leaf clover," he said. "It hardly ever happens." Ekta beamed with satisfaction.

Journal: Thursday, or maybe Wednesday

Michael had a rough day, came home tired and sad. A nineteen year-old patient had just died. He had crashed his motorcycle driving at eighty miles per hour.

These days I seem to want to impress in my children's minds the consequences of bad decisions—especially foolish decisions made by teenagers who somehow feel invincible against tragic odds. I don't worry too much about Benjamin because he is such a wise old soul, always conservative and steady. Ekta, though, is a wildly free spirit, a spontaneous crowd pleaser, and a girl! I do worry about peer pressure. And so I said, "Ekta, I hope you would never ride on a motorcycle like that. Even if it was your favorite boyfriend and he drove up to you and said, 'Hop up behind me and hold on. I'll take you for a ride.' I hope you would tell him no thanks."

She turned her innocent face to me, smiling. "Oh Mom, I could *never* say that." My hopes fell. "If he told me to do something that stupid I'd tell him, 'I'm no longer taken with you. Scat!'"

What a gem! I'll have to remember that line. Michael said he could have used it at least six times today.

Journal: Friday, the last day of soccer camp

When Mary Ellen brought the children home this afternoon, she told me a funny story. She said the camp director started out this last day of camp by gathering everyone for a meeting. He began with an announcement that the lost-and-found had collected many items over the week and he wanted to find out who the owners were. So, he said, please raise your hand if you've lost anything this week. Mary Ellen said that Ekta raised her hand immediately and he called on her first.

"I lost my tooth," she said proudly.

I was happy that Mary Ellen stopped to chat. Always grateful for her cheerful company, I especially needed a good laugh at that moment. I was despairing over the flower arrangements I was trying to prepare for Monday's fundraising dinner. My mother and I had had a rather frustrating day collecting supplies, and I was starting to worry. The bugs were moving into the white roses, and my peonies were clearly not going to last until Monday, their lovely petals floating away in the breezes, one by one.

Journal: Saturday or Sunday

It seems that when I have a big project with lots of lists to do and things to collect and decisions to make, my mind gets a little out of control and stuff gets badly jumbled. I do lose a lot of sleep over it. I remember this happened with the church play last February, and it's happening again. I don't seem to get the sequence and timing straight, so even when something is already completed my mind seems to be processing and reprocessing over and over as if the decision is yet to be made, or the task has not yet been done. All the extra data bouncing around up there needs to be continually reconsidered, then stored or eliminated. I get stuck in a mess of data and details that confuse me during the day and wake me in a panic at night.

My mother suggests that I might need to "close the file," like we do with the computer before turning it off, so that it shuts down properly.

Journal: After July 5th

Guess it's after July 5, because I just poured sour milk out of a jug marked July 5 into my tea. The calendar tells me it is 9 July 2000 and my eyes tell me it's another gray, cold, summer day. My spirits are as gloomy as the weather. My head aches. I'm dizzy, shaky, and exhausted. It's only eight in the morning. Michael's at the clinic all day and I don't know what I'll be able to manage with the children. Of course Benjamin will want to read all day, the latest hair-raising escapades of Harry Potter, but that means Ekta has no playmate. And I don't have the energy for exuberant chatter and projects.

I'm so sick of this brain injury!! Several weeks ago, I was contemplating an overnight birthday party in New Hampshire. Ekta and I both had been invited to her friend's birthday celebration, a slumber party with hiking, swimming, cave exploring, and mini golf. Mary Ellen said she would drive my van. Both she and Helen would be there to help. I really wanted to try it and was talking through the details with my mother. As she expressed her many concerns, I got really frustrated and raised my voice in a loud protest. "I'm not going to be a prisoner to this brain injury forever!"

I think my words startled us both. My mother had very legitimate concerns about my capabilities—whether I could physically handle the trip—and even greater concerns about what might happen to me emotionally if things didn't go well or if unknowing people made insensitive comments. Some statements seem so simple yet can be devastating to my spirit and leave me feeling misunderstood and isolated.

The truth is, though, I am a stranger. Somehow I need to re-enter my world.

And this morning, July 9, I feel like a prisoner again, my choices so limited by my state of mind and physical energy. Yet I can choose my attitude. So with the ease that comes from much practice, I slip into my survival mantra: *patience and gratitude, acceptance and hope*. Over and over again I say the words to myself. They are well-worn and comfortable, like the slipper-socks that I have pretty much lived in since the injury. Now the socks have a hole in the heel of the left foot, the foot I always used to find the edge of the stairs before stepping down with my stronger right leg. It took a very long time of doing stairs in that fashion to actually make this hole. I realized recently that I can often go down stairs now in a rather normal manner. *Patience and gratitude.*

Yet days like this are so disappointing. Days like this, I sit with a pile of clean laundry, lacking enough mental voltage to figure out how to sort it, fold it, and deliver it to the right rooms. The kitchen is a mess. Who ever would have thought that dishwashing is a brainy task? Days like this, I wish my dear mother were here—straightening, organizing, cleaning—blessing us like an angel. Yet at the same time, I don't want her here. I don't want to have to need her help.

I burst into tears with the realization that I still can't manage our household and my children's lives for more than a few days at a time before I crumble with mindlessness and fatigue. I feel ill, and I feel like a failure. Asking for help just underscores those sentiments—puts them in bold print, all caps: **INCOMPETENT**.

One truly amazing thing, though, is that I'm actually writing these thoughts!! I'm having them and holding onto them long enough to make a record. Now that actually is a tremendously miraculous breakthrough. I can't believe it. This is the first time I've ever been able to write when I feel like this. OK. *Patience and gratitude, acceptance and hope.*

Writing is such a complex process, cognitively speaking. Things must be getting better if I'm actually doing this.

E-mail: To Christin
Date: Sometime in July

Christin, dear one,

I started writing in my journal again!!

The first time was during our trip to Maine. We stayed

at a bed-and-breakfast inn during our summer trip. Other years we've always done the bed-and-breakfast overnight in conjunction with a longer period of camping out. This year we skipped the camping. After we had returned home, Ekta said to me with a sort of alarmed look on her face, "Oh no, Mom—we forgot to go to Maine this summer." It was sort of like the way she says, "Oh no, Mom—you forgot to pick up Benjamin," when I drive past the place I'm supposed to get him, not remembering where I'm going.

I said, "We did go to Maine, honey, remember? You and Daddy made the great big sandcastle, and Benjamin froze in all those bodysurfing waves. We stayed at the bed-and-breakfast and you had your own little bed."

"Oh yeah, now I remember," she said. "But it didn't feel like Maine, when we go camping at Hermit Island."

"Right," I said. "We decided to do it a little differently this year." I didn't add, "That's because Mom needs far more sleep than one can generally count on while camping (even if I could find my way to the bathroom and back in the middle of the night). And I would barely be able to get one bag packed—never mind an entire car full of groceries and gear."

Ekta said something about liking the bed-and-breakfast because the bugs were better, but I missed the rest because my mind wandered off to previous summer trips to Maine.

I have a very clear picture of myself a couple years ago. A few hours before we were to leave home, I was standing on our deck simultaneously keeping an eye on my little ones playing in the pond and the veggie chili that I was preparing for a camping dinner, concocted without a recipe, the way I always cooked. In addition, I was doing a final check of our gear to be sure we had all we'd need—and more. The standing joke in our camping crew was that PJ never forgets a thing, so if you don't have what you need just go to her tent; you'll find it there. And the whole time I was on the telephone trying to work out a potentially homicidal crisis with a client—making calls to her, the police, and the psychologist who would be covering my practice while I was camping. Michael had not yet gotten home so I was on my own, getting everything taken care of. I felt busy, yet pretty comfortable with all of it, capable anyway.

When I started my rehab with Lakshmi, I told her about that day, and how different it was to even think about going on a camping trip this year and that it seemed pretty impossible to expect to enjoy it. I said, "Right now I can't do even one of those things well. In the old days I did them easily, all at the same time, without any recipes, lists, notes, or worries that I'd miss something really big—like forgetting to keep an eye on my children in the pond."

E-mail: To Christin
Date: Sometime in July

Ekta is going to animal camp this week at the Humane Society shelter. She is their guest speaker on Monday and is taking our chickens, Snowy and Sunflower, and maybe the three young hatchlings, Pepperpot, Pearly-Girl, and Buffy Blue-Feet. The big hens will have to stay home because they aren't particularly sociable with strangers. On Thursday, Ekta returns to camp with Naisa, our miniature Nigerian dairy goat, who actually will never be a milker because she's a teeny runt, entirely too small to breed.

The animals have been precious to me in my recovery, especially Bravo, who rode home from the miniature horse farm in the back seat of our van. He joined our family the evening before Ekta's birthday. That was Benjamin's idea, to sneak Bravo into the horse stall and surprise Ekta the next morning when she went down for barn chores. Someday I would like to write about animals and healing, and the many blessings of barn life, especially manure.

There is so much in your letters that I want to respond to but can't quite yet—things I can't seem to "wrap my brain around." Please know that the questions are precious to me though, all of them. Often my thoughts take a long time before they find a way into words. Before my injury I used to think in words, talk to myself in words very quickly. It's different now.

You said that I am sounding fantastic. "Your writing remains beautiful, with smooth phrasing."

Well, the e-mail printouts make me sound pretty good! You don't see the many, many long pauses, scribbles, and arrows you would see on paper. My computer gets impatient, though. It tells me every few minutes that I have been inactive and asks if I wish to remain online. That question makes me nervous. If I don't process it correctly, I lose everything I have been laboring to get to you through the wires. I would like to tell my computer that I'm just dancing a while under the stars, looking for a word in the wildflower jungle of my mind.

However, I don't think that would work. So when I'm having a particularly slow and jumbled mind, I write in my journal, then send that on the e-mail. That works better, and I can write in the sun, smelling the sultry sumptuous milkweed in full bloom at the meadow's edge.

And by the way, I told Ekta about your kitten. She asked its name, and I said it might be T.S. Eliot. "I like that name," she said. "T.S. probably stands for Sneaky Timmy."

Journal: Sometime between Helen's dinner
and our Duluth trip

Yesterday, I drove the twelve miles to Hardwick to pick up Benjin from Alicia's house; she had taken the boys to summer hockey in Montpelier. That was the first time I'd driven to Hardwick since leaving my office last September. Ekta was in the car, and as we passed through Main Street, she said, "Look, Mom, there's your office." I scanned the names that hang on shingles from the Threshold Counseling and Bodywork sign on the building. Mine was still hanging there, along with the other names. I was relieved that they hadn't taken it down. Somebody else was renting my office, but I don't know if I was ready to see my name gone from the sign. I had a rush of feelings I wasn't prepared to deal with and was grateful for the traffic light changing at that moment, requiring my concentration to move through the intersection.

As we headed out of town toward Alicia's, Ekta said, "Remember, Mom, when Haley and I came to work with you that day and you gave us two dollars to go to the store? We went by ourselves and bought ice cream and we sat on your office steps and ate it?"

I know that was only last summer, but it felt like a lifetime away. I was climbing over a lot of dusty boxes in my memory attic, to a dark corner with a forgotten trunk. "I do remember that, honey. I had a meeting upstairs, and you girls got Peace Pops."

"Yeah, that was fun. I'd like to do that again. Do you think you'll ever go back to your office?" That's the question that haunts me—the one I don't want to have to answer—because right now the answer is not one I like.

"I don't know, darling. I certainly hope so, but I'm not sure." We were winding north along the river. I focused on the boulders, as I sometimes do when I need to draw upon strength that is greater than my own, strength that endures in spite of erosion.

"You like helping people, don't you, Mom? That's why you do that kind of work? Because you like to help your clients with problems?"

"That's right, Ekta. That's what I like to do."

I thought about the conversation Michael and I had just recently about renewing my professional liability insurance. I thought it seemed rather pointless to pay the premium if I wasn't going to work with clients. But Michael said it makes sense to pay it until we know for sure whether I'll be returning to my work in any capacity. And so the next morning I dug through my "Work" basket—still in its same place under the kitchen phone—and looked for my insurance renewal form and my state license. I had those weird feelings of dislocation, like the time last winter when my mother and I cleaned out my home office. Now I felt like I was going through somebody else's stuff again.

Journal: Some day in July

Christin has finished reading Claudia Osborn's book *Over My Head*. She's a doctor who was brain-injured in a bike accident, and her book describes the rehab she went through. Now that Christin has a better understanding of what a brain-injured person goes through, she is wondering how much of Claudia's experience is similar to mine. I haven't actually read the book myself, so I can't say. When Michael asked all our family members to read the book, it was because so much of her story did seem to be like my own. There were times when he read passages to me that sounded like they would have come out of my own mouth, if only I had been able to articulate what was happening with me.

I do remember thinking how much it helped to hear her describe experiences that I shared but couldn't express in words even to myself, never mind to anyone else. The one thing Michael always said to me was that her injury involved brain stem damage and mine did not, thank God. So my prognosis, hopefully, is better. I remain optimistic.

Recently I started reading parts of her book, and I hope to continue in small bits. One thing that amazed me was her ability to recall and write a detailed sequence of events. I couldn't even begin to follow her first chapters—all her comings and goings here and there—leading up to and following her accident, her arrival in New York, and entrance into rehab. Of course just now as I am writing this I realize that I could probably recall and record the events leading up to my own accident. I could also recall the events following the accident and the couple of days before the swelling in my brain forced me to bed for the next several months. The part I can't write about very well is what I call "the dark time"—the period when my mind did not seem to work at all, was completely empty, and I slept close to twenty hours of every twenty-four. That's why it was dark. I also remember that I couldn't handle much stimulation, so it was a very silent time as well.

Perhaps that's why I wouldn't be able to write much. Not much happened, except sleeping and silence.

2

Pomegranates and Figs

E-mail: To Christin
Date: Before Duluth

Christin dearest,

Next week we're going to Duluth to visit Michael's parents and to go to his twenty-fifth high school reunion. What a huge undertaking for me—trying to plan, organize, pack. I'm very tired and somewhat apprehensive about the whole thing.

I wanted to say how reassuring your last e-mail was. Your lovely words lead me to many thoughts and images that I am eager to share, though I am frustrated because the process of articulating is so difficult. Yet I do seem to be able to journal fairly well now, not so bothered by all the crossing out.

What you wrote was really hopeful, especially the part where you suggested that "the process of crossing off and scribbling and arrows pointing here and there is a manifestation of the brain's finding new pathways and ways of organizing. This is probably a picture of your healing. And look at what you end up with! Beautiful and smooth phrasing. Wow! This is a fantastic accomplishment."

Thanks for that message. And so much love to you.

Journal: Duluth, Minnesota, Monday morning

This is the second Monday morning that I've woken and known what day it is and my schedule, too. The first time that I awoke and knew the day was Ekta's first morning of animal camp. That was July 17, exactly ten months after my accident. What a major accomplishment to get out of bed knowing the day of the week and the time of day!

Last week was exhausting, preparing for our trip to Duluth, but what I accomplished was a sign of truly remarkable progress in my recovery. Thankfully, as usual, my mother was willing to help out. Things were well-managed using my conversation notebook and daily basket, but my energy was not strong. Lakshmi suggested that I take sticky notes down to the barn and leave them wherever I do something that needs to be explained to the caretakers. With those concrete markers in place I could more easily write directions, get the sequence right, and not leave anything out.

It turned out to be an extremely challenging but profitable exercise. I'm thankful for the practical help I get through my rehab and cognitive retraining. It enables me to function with more confidence and less anxiety. Even though some of the steps probably seem cumbersome to an onlooker, and I do sometimes feel like a robot, for me it's the ticket to a measure of independence.

My mother has said that maybe she should have a book and a basket system, too. Michael calls my notebook my "peripheral brain." He said that in medical training all the residents had them always close at hand for the information they needed in emergencies and hadn't yet internalized. Now, of course, such information is a part of Michael, something known in his muscles and marrow, something like breathing. Perhaps, as I work with my notebook and baskets—my peripheral brain—my own brain will re-create a sorting, filing, and storage system, and if I'm lucky, it too will become automatic.

Surely my sense of time will be restored. As Christin pointed out, children don't get a sense of historical flow until a certain age, so it's developmental. I remember when Benjamin was little he always referred to any time other than the present as "tomorrow after that day." I loved the way he said it, the creative workings of his little brain as it grappled with the mysteries of time that we grown-ups take for granted.

Young children live so beautifully in the experience of the present. As I write this, Ekta is skipping stones into Lake Superior, stones made silky smooth through eons of pounding, crashing turbulence. And I sit in a cozy nook where craggy jagged rock ledges have soaked up the sun's heat for centuries of summers. Ekta can't beat her record of twelve skips from a single stone, so she has abandoned that challenge for the new adventure of discovering well-worn beach glass. She tells me that it comes from the green and brown bottles of whiskey-drinking pirates!

Michael and I went to dinner last night at Bennett's on the Lake. He had walleye and I had lamb. He drank a bottle of wine by himself because I'm still not drinking alcohol or caffeine—nothing to alter my brain any more than it's already altered. The waiter came and recited the dessert choices much too fast for me, and there were too many. I asked him to give us a minute to think about it. When he left I asked Michael about something with dates and walnuts—what was that? He looked surprised; he said there hadn't been anything like that, and we both started to laugh.

"Oh God," I said. "This feels like the testing with Dr. Drudge. He goes through a list of words and then asks me to recite those I remember. Vegetables and fruits was one category, and I always came up with rutabagas and pomegranates, neither of which he had said. He was impressed, though! He had never gotten that one before. Then he told me about growing up on the Michigan peninsula in a little town that had a rutabaga festival every year."

I said to Michael, "Let's order rutabagas and pomegranates." He ordered cappuccino cheesecake and asked the waiter if there was something with dates.

"No dates," the waiter replied, "but there is a fig tart."

Now Michael hadn't even registered that one: he doesn't like figs. "Isn't it interesting how quickly we filter out what we don't have a receptor site for?" he said. He remembered a favorite doctor in medical training who said, "The eye does not see what the mind does not know."

At the time of my neuropsych evaluation, I was trying to relearn the grocery store, starting with produce. I hadn't made much progress in several attempts, but I at least had those rutabagas and pomegranates down. Since then, my mother developed a perfectly wonderful system for my meal planning and grocery shopping, and I have to say that I'm delighted with my progress in that department. I track my shopping accomplishments by how many dollars' worth of the correct food supplies I can purchase at a time. Maybe that sounds funny, but it means successfully planning the meals, making the ingredient list, driving to the store, finding my way through the aisles and checkout, making it home again with everything, and putting it away where I'll find it again. No more ice cream in the washing machine or toothpaste in the fridge. My last receipt, for $160, was a record.

My meals and baking are all planned out to the letter. There is nothing spontaneous in my kitchen anymore, quite unlike the old me who never used a recipe. It's against my grain to be so confined! But it's OK. I think of what Christin said about missing the water after she moved from her old house: "I can't see any water from the house. A loss for me. And no voluptuous lemon tree either! But I had those things once as part of my life, and now I have something else."

I think that's a fine way to put it all in perspective: *Now I have something else.*

Journal: Thursday afternoon in Vermont, August 3, right after we returned from Minnesota

Accurately reporting both the day and the date. WOW. And very pleased to note that my awareness of date is in large part due to the work I have just successfully completed with getting my computer hitched up to the bank. I can now see and print out all the things I used to struggle to figure out with impatient tellers in confusing phone conversations. I know, for example, that Michael's paycheck was just deposited today, April third. And I no longer will worry about mishaps, forgotten entries, and transposed figures in the checking account.

We had a tremendous thunder and lightning storm when I first was going through the set-up and I was not successful, but the customer service rep said that it was probably weather-related and to try again later. Voila, it worked! I am thinking about all the delays on our homeward flights and feeling relieved that we arrived safely. It's a bit unnerving to consider how delicate the computer circuits are, and how susceptible to interference from lightning bolts and other bits of celestial chaos.

My friend Helen once said, "There's nothing better than coming home."

I replied, "The only thing better is never to have left in the first place." I sure am getting firmly anchored.

Buffy Blue-Feet's fatal accident made for a grim homecoming. Scurrying into the coop with the other chickens, she had gotten underfoot of the caretaker, who ended up stepping on her head. Ekta wanted to know exactly when she had died, hoping that she died at night while she was asleep, because going to sleep is the best way to die. Benjin assured her that even if Buffy died during the day, the bleeding in her head put her to sleep first.

Ekta chose the spot to bury her, in the little chicken yard where Buffy and the other babies had played around the poplar sapling. I was amazed at how comfortable Ekta was holding Buffy, petting her and laying her in the hole Michael had dug. Benjin, who has no stomach for such things, watched from a safe distance until all was done, but Ekta needed to experience it intimately: caressing, smelling, making a grass bed and pillow, covering Buffy with soil, finding a large rock, and cutting special flowers. Tonight we'll all look for Buffy's star in the sky.

I'm home alone today on the couch while a summer shower soaks the earth. Sometimes it's hard to be alone, especially if I don't feel well enough to do anything, but today I'm enjoying the solitude. I spent much of the morning working on deduction puzzles, my "homework" from rehab. I'm improving, but I do still get stuck. If I have to hold something in my head because there is no obvious "box" to put it in and several possibilities need to be ruled out, I get hopelessly tangled up. Then, by the time I've gotten one piece sorted out, I've lost the others.

I imagine this kind of mental gymnastics is doing something for me, but I'm not sure exactly what. I do realize that

I'm "thinking." In other words, I'm attaching meaning to concepts and shifting them around in my head. There is energy and movement to that. It's an odd sensation, not something I experienced before my injury.

Learning higher math required a similar mental manipulation. Don't they insist that algebra teaches us to think? But these "puzzles" now are with language, which was always so fluent and automatic for me. Now I struggle over sentences like, "The singer gives his wife flowers in September," or "Daffodils are given by someone other than the doctor." I spent the morning deciphering sentences like that, seven of them, searching for clues so I could fill in a simple chart showing which professional gave what kind of flower to his wife in which month.

E-mail: To Christin
Date: After Duluth

We've been home three weeks and this morning I woke up feeling rested and clear for the first time since our return. I'm also relaxed because Michael is off this weekend (he's worked the last two and so was completely unavailable to us). I have a different ease and energy when I know that I'm not entirely on my own. I don't have to be so careful, managing my activities so that I will last through all that I have to be "up" for. When my fatigue starts to take over and my mind gets all fuzzy, I start to feel like an injured animal acts—surly and protective, sending out "stay away from me" messages.

You can imagine that's not at all the way I like to be around my children (or anyone, for that matter, though I'm generally not around other people these days). I worry that I won't hold up long enough to carry through on whatever it is that needs doing—feeding them or driving them here and there. It's always a relief to have my mother here for that reason, among many others. And when Michael is here I don't have to be so disciplined, so I am liberated to enjoy what I'm doing without trying to think about what comes next and whether I can last. It's a special sense of freedom with him.

I really like that line from your letter: "Please rest and know that you have your whole life, so you don't have to hurry up with anything. The healing comes no matter what you do, I feel certain of that." I've said that to myself a million times since I read it. Sometimes I don't rest very well because I am so annoyed that I *need* to rest. My frustration and disappointment get the better of me. I'd like to be capable of hurrying up with a lot of things (even just one would be nice), but that's not my tempo just now, and everything is better when I honor that instead of resisting it.

I've started taking photographs around my home and gardens. I do it in my really slow times—my no-thought, no-energy times when the thing I do best is sit still and look around me. I began photographing by accident after some disappointing moments this summer with gardening.

In the late winter, I realized that very little of my former life was available to me. I couldn't re-enter my work, committees, or the brainy relationships and activities that had been so much a part of me. I was looking out the window, thinking that my gardens were inviting me back to them, brain injury or not, and it was sustaining to look forward to doing something so familiar that I could do it and feel like my "real" self.

I hadn't done any of the autumn clean-up or spring-time preparation, though, and became overwhelmed by the amount of work that the gardens needed, compounded by my lack of physical energy. Often I would go out with my weeding bucket, clippers, tools, and good intentions. After what seemed like a forever of working, but was in fact only a few minutes, I'd realize that I was too tired and would just sit there. Unable to do much thinking, I began to do some pretty profound looking. One day, it occurred to me that I was seeing images I'd never seen before, because I'd never been still long enough.

I've begun to see beautiful pictures, the kind you see in those luxurious coffee-table books. So now, instead of going to the garden with a bucket full of tools, I take just one (usually clippers for deadheading) and I take my camera. I'm making cards from the photographs. I want to ask my friends to send them to people who are lonely, hurt, sick, forgotten, or weary with the world. I remember how much it meant to me to receive cards with lovely images and colors when I was convalescing in the early days after my injury, during the time when I felt so awful physically and so incapable mentally. In one of my awake moments I said to myself, "What have I learned from this experience that I never want to forget?"

As the weeks went on, different things came to me, and one was this: Whenever someone is hurting, send a card or note. Send something tangible and beautiful that a person can hold and look at, can read over and over again. It really matters. It makes a difference, seeing that you are being held in someone's thoughts. Don't say, "I'll do it later" or "I'm no good with words" or "I'm too busy and now it's so late." Just put something in the mail.

I never want to forget that. I asked my mom and Michael to remember it for me, so when I am better I will still know it.

I like the way photographing my flowers actually makes me slow down even more. Sometimes I have to wait a very long time for a certain picture because a tiny breeze has moved things out of focus or a bug landed in the wrong place or a cloud just passed over the sun and now I have to wait for the light rays to be just right again. The healing does continue no matter what, and I don't have to hurry up with anything. Those words you wrote, dear Christin, are precious to me, and my gardens are the perfect metaphor.

I've come a long way in terms of grieving the loss and accepting this brain injury. But I'd really like to build a more solid self-awareness and sense of competence. It seems like there are still many unknowns—too many holes and question marks when I look in the mirror.

I'd like to know the components of an "intensive, structured, rehabilitation program." That's what my evaluations say I need. Lakshmi explained that my higher-level skills are not available to me because of cracks in the foundation that would allow me to access and utilize them. What exactly are those cracks in my cognitive foundation? How do I mend them?

It's the seemingly "little things" that are not quite right, that have major manifestations in functioning. After Michael read Claudia Osborn's book, he said to Melissa, my primary care doctor, "These are tiny things that are wrong, but they are tiny things with a huge impact."

I read and reread my evaluation reports, but they don't give me the answers I seek. There is something very limiting about testing. I can't actually wrap my brain around what I'm trying to express here, so will have to try again later. But one thing I know is that when I'm able to repeat accurately, although very slowly, one sentence spoken directly to me alone in a slow, deliberate manner in a totally quiet testing room, all we can say is that I did exactly that. We can't assume that I can then listen to the ticketing agent at the airline counter rattle off directions in a noisy airport with a mob of people and expect that I'll find my departure gate unaided. Or that I can recall a sentence spoken an hour ago, when I'm driving and Benjamin asks what time Katharine said she'd meet us. That one almost caused a terrific collision as I focused on his question and started to pull out into traffic, looking only to my right. Benjamin hollered just in time for me to brake.

I wish I knew a little more about what needs repairing and how to retrain/relearn. I think I could make further progress if I only knew what exactly is wrong. Dr. Drudge's report states that my "spontaneous recovery" is nearing an end. I still see progress every few weeks; however, that may be from adaptations and accommodations rather than healing/recovery. Lakshmi says she never tells a patient they have reached their "plateau," because she believes the brain is always creating new pathways. It takes time.

Yesterday I was thinking about how I don't really care for those instant, tidy gardens that look as if they were plopped down by machines instead of growing up from the earth. I'd rather see the young plants and saplings, even if they look too small at first, knowing that they'll be well-rooted over time.

So often, people seem to be merely skimming the surface of life, impatiently speeding along. Yet if we slow down, go a little deeper, we tap into those wellsprings that have endured for centuries. Out of patience and faith, we grow much stronger. That's what I like to remind myself these days. "You don't have to hurry up with anything" is great advice for both healing and landscaping.

3

Morning Glory

Journal: August 2000

This past week I had an appointment scheduled to see Lakshmi. My mother came up the night before, as she always does, to drive me to Burlington (an hour away) and take care of Benjamin and Ekta while I'm at the hospital. They dropped me off, and when I went inside to check in, the receptionist said Lakshmi is on vacation this week.

"You must have the date wrong," they told me.

"No," I said. "This is what I wrote down while the woman was talking on the phone to me." That's what I do now, in my conversation notebook, so I know that she said Lakshmi's vacation had changed, and this is the week I was supposed to be here. I also said that I had just gotten a call from the hospital yesterday reconfirming my appointment for today.

This was one of those all-too-familiar mix-ups that I have experienced because of my inability and mistakes, but I was hoping that for once I had gotten it right. As I stood there, I realized thankfully that I was not flooding—overwhelmed by confusion and awash in my emotions. That's what usually happens when I have to think quickly. Instead, I got out my notebook and looked up my telephone conversation with the appointments woman. Then the receptionist checked her schedule on the computer and although one part did show that Lakshmi was on vacation this week, another part showed that I was in fact scheduled for an eleven o'clock appointment and that a reconfirmation call had been made the day before. My annoyance over the inconvenience paled in light of my great triumph. For once I had gotten it right!

I suppose that seems like a trivial thing, but as I gain competence, I also must increase my confidence. So it's actually extremely helpful when somebody says, "You've got that exactly right. It's my mistake, not yours."

Michael has been immensely helpful in that department. He seems to have a keen awareness of the role confidence plays in successful use of our skills. (He says it certainly makes a difference in his doctoring.) Most of the time he is the first to tell me when mishaps are his doing, not mine. That's pretty noble in a spouse, I think. There have been times, though, when we've had some real doozies.

I remember him once saying that a great benefit of my injury is that we argue less now. I'm actually incapable of processing words quickly enough to argue. It's very painstaking and slow if we have to work out a difference, because I have to take notes and he has to repeat things many times. That's an arduous way to argue, and few things are worth that much effort—an indication of how many marital squabbles probably are quite unnecessary.

I remember getting really upset one time, though, because I just wanted to be able to be right about something for once, deftly prove my point, and have him admit that my way was at least admirable, if not superior. A funny thing to get upset over, really, but it is nice to feel right some of the time, even about things that don't matter all that much.

So I was happy on Tuesday when I had to wait at the hospital during my cancelled appointment. I went out to a sunny bench, next to a small bed of fragrant annuals by the patient entrance. The scheduling mix-up meant that I now had an hour to see what I usually don't see at rehab—all the other patients coming and going, many in wheelchairs or on stretchers. I thank God I'm not going to rehab to learn how to live without my legs or with only one arm, or to learn to talk through a machine or with my eyes because they're the only part of my body that I can move.

I met a woman on the plane to Minnesota. She told me that because of a pesticide poisoning accident, she had lost all ability to smell and taste. I'm thinking about that as I sit here cherishing the garden scents beside me, the pungent marigolds and deliciously sweet alyssum. I can't imagine living without smell and taste, sight, sound—any of it.

She said, "You learn to live with what you've got."

"Yes," I agreed. "I guess we're all invited to do that."

Gretchen is in her garden as I write today. Last week was the first time she went to work without a hat. Her radiated scalp is starting to grow the tiniest bit of hair. I wonder if her expectation to live and her dream of birthing a child are starting to grow the tiniest bit of hope in her heart. I don't know how someone lives fully with the threat of recurring cancer. Of course, everything does become more precious, and perhaps one lives more fully than ever.

In your last e-mail, you were mentioning a spiritual teacher you know: "She claims to have the same experience of present moment awareness as you do, with virtually no connection between that moment and the past or future. Lots of spiritual traditions think of this as a very high state of consciousness."

Yes, I suppose it is. Mind you, it isn't one I choose to be in perpetually, although there is tremendous tranquility there, and profound "seeing" into the moment. I do remember sitting in my bed shortly after the accident, looking out the window, and watching the same tree branches day after day. There were absolutely no thoughts in my head, and I couldn't have found one no matter how hard I tried. It was autumn time—the colors changing slowly, at a pace I could take in, when there was very little else I could keep up with.

My moment to moment existence (when I wasn't in physical pain or sleeping) was quite blissful during those periods. I felt altered, closer to God, and very much held by love. I didn't know it in my head because I was not capable of thinking about it, but I felt it—my bones knew it.

One November morning I opened the blinds in the upstairs bathroom window and looked down on the pergola that covers part of the deck. The morning glories that had been so bountiful throughout the summer twisted and turned their curly vines all over the top of the pergola. By now, of course, most of them had turned crispy and brown. A light snow had fallen during the night, bringing just enough moisture to one delicate green tendril, and the brilliantly warm sun had coaxed out a single star-faced, cloudy blue blossom.

Though I have no recollection of so much from that period of time, that last lovely kiss of summer in the middle of

November's snow is etched in my memory forever. And the absolute purity and vivid oneness of the moment is something I cherish.

Yet having said that, I must also be very frank in admitting that it is not a place I'd like to stay, not right now. It's like an island, cut off from the rest of the world. I like the way Anne Morrow Lindbergh described island living in *Gift from the Sea*. She wrote that one exists only in the present tense. Cut off from the future and the past, you live in the here and now, like a child or a saint.

But I would not like to be stranded on the island forever. A friend said to me that she thinks my recovery experience sounds like a Buddhist breakthrough—or something like that. I didn't have my conversation notebook then and don't know what her exact words were. I think there's a difference, though. I don't know if the monks are ever so deeply in the other world of present moment that they can't return to this world and do what needs doing. I am very grateful to have had the incredible experience and also now to be recovering from it, or perhaps a better word is returning from it.

But I'm not really returning. I'm going someplace else.

E-mail: To Christin
Date: August 26, 2000

Christin dear, I am sorry to know you are temporarily bedridden. I'm hoping John will bring roses to your bedside. If I were closer, I'd bring rose water for your pillowcase and some of my tea—wintergreen and lemon verbena would be just right—because of course sleep is such a good thing but doesn't always come easily.

In your last e-mail, you said something about the voices chattering in your already-cacophonous head. That made me remember when some of my concussion began to abate—

how I would have terrible anxiety because out of my sleep, voices would start chattering. They weren't really "voices," because that implies an ego, and I didn't have much of one then. Rather, they were a cacophony of random, noisy little bits of thoughts that came incoherently in fits and spurts with data, information, and pieces of old "to-do" lists—everything out of context and jumbled in time and space.

My brain would wake me in the middle of my sleep with these things loudly crashing into each other. Traveling from far off like comets from ancient galaxies, gaining momentum as they come to incarnate in my cerebral gel, they would compete for space there in the tiny spot that was just barely remembering how to work, and explode like meteors.

My joy over realizing that there was still something "up there"—when all had been empty and silent for so long—was too easily extinguished by my excruciating fatigue which, as you can imagine, took quite a turn for the worse with all the sleep interruptions. Also, I didn't have the cognitive ability to order the jumbled data and reconcile the dissonance. And I was anxious and disturbed, wondering if this was to be the extent of my recovery.

I so much want to write more, but can't right now, so I will put this in the "wait to send" box and set my kitchen clock so that I don't forget it's in here. Then if the timer goes off before I write more, at least I'll send this much.

Till then, I love you and hope you are feeling so much better.

E-MAIL: TO CHRISTIN
DATE: SEPTEMBER 3, 2000

Christin dearest:

I would like to be more timely and consistent in my correspondence with you. I am wondering if, when the children are back in school during the day, my energy will be more available to me, or whether that will just mean a different, equally demanding schedule. I guess I'll just have to wait and see.

I am starting to feel a little frustrated with the number of notes to myself that are accumulating, because I worry that when I finally feel up to working with them I'll not find words for the many things I want to write about. At least now, though, I have a workable system for my notes. And it's better than it used to be, when I'd jot words on a notepad or scrap of paper, hoping to remind myself of something important or to prepare for a conversation. But later, when I'd refer back to them, the notes wouldn't make sense. Often I couldn't even find the scraps of paper. Of course, over time I have learned how to write myself better notes, and I've become very organized about placing them in my daily basket or conversation notebook, but that is through a long process of rehabilitation, not something I stumbled upon spontaneously.

I guess I'll simply need to trust that whatever happens will be right. In the meantime, I'll keep writing these grace notes and try to enjoy the fact that I am having so many thoughts knitting together quite nicely in response to your writings. Maybe it doesn't really matter if this new dance in my head leaves no evidence on paper for a long time, or ever.

E-MAIL: TO CHRISTIN
DATE: SEPTEMBER 4, 2000

Good morning lovely Christin,

I have been thinking about the intimacy we can achieve through our e-mail "conversations." It seems to have to do with the pace and the silence. The silence, shorter than with mailed letters, allows me to slowly absorb meaning while not losing connections. And I'm not rushed or interrupted as I am with face to face or phone conversation.

When you asked if I remember how it used to be for me before my accident, the picture that comes into my mind is one of me standing before a class of college students, teaching psychology and communication courses. I am directing them through a sequence of exercises leading to the discovery that the mind listens at a much faster rate than it speaks. I can't recall exactly how many words per minute you can hear and comprehend versus how many you can formulate and express, but there is a great disparity. This is why when someone is talking we often think we know what they're going to say before the words come out of their mouth, and we start formulating a response. Or we get lost in our own musings: how that person looks, what we'll eat for dinner, or myriad other random, daydreaming thoughts. Our brains are wired to process speech at a rapid rate, far faster than the speaker's pace, and so we must discipline ourselves to use the "spare time" constructively.

Another picture I have is one of sitting with couples in marriage counseling sessions and realizing that although one partner is working diligently to accurately reflect the other's words, he or she is completely unable to process the meaning. I always thought this had to do with emotional interference—an inability to process the meaning because it is too painful or it doesn't jibe with "my side of the story." But the more I have come to experience my own struggles with auditory processing, the greater my insight into some fascinating phenomena. I think I told you that I am unable to argue. There are many dimensions, or perhaps cognitive skills, required to debate successfully, and they are beyond me. For one, I get stuck because I can't hold onto the other person's words and thoughts accurately or long enough to formulate a response. They come in to me all jumbled up and confused.

Listening is not just a "hearing" thing, but a "mind" thing. As Benjamin said the other day, so accurately, "I think my ears are bigger than my mind." In other words, the ears can take in a great quantity, but the mind may not be able to process it all. And because all language is metaphor—a symbolic representation of thought—it's not enough to simply hear the words with your ears (i.e., grasp the surface structure). In order to listen and converse, you must get hold of the deeper structure and process the *concept* that the words symbolize. Sometimes I have to repeat short phrases of a statement over and over to myself out loud before I actually "hear" the message or get the point. The process of learning how to listen successfully again has led me to a greater understanding of Benjamin's difficulties with auditory processing.

I am particularly excited about the possibility of working with Dr. Musiek (pronounced "music"), an audiologist at Dartmouth. One of the original pioneers in the field, he's been researching central auditory processing for about twenty years. I am hopeful that he will be able to help both Benjamin and me. My mother found an article about his work and was attracted to it because of his success with brain-injured and stroke patients. As she read on, the boy in the article sounded to her a lot like Benjamin. The more I learn, the more I see similarities in certain challenges that both of us face.

Of course, a significant difference between Benjamin and me is that for all of my life prior to my injury, I was a superb auditory processor. That was probably one of the gifts that led to my counseling and consulting work, and my interest in helping people to enrich relationships through improved interpersonal communication. I remember very well how natural and easy it was for me to accurately listen to and retain not just one person's story, but that of several people at a time, as in conflict resolution and mediation work. Technically speaking, the normally-functioning mind is equipped to do that, and with training I had become quite accomplished at it.

I am still saddened by this loss. Obviously, without it, my professional work is beyond my reach. But more than that, I grieve not being able to tune in successfully to my children (or to Michael or friends) in a reliable manner. I remember sitting on the couch with Benjamin last year, talking about how everybody has special gifts. He said, "You're really the best listener, Mom. Nobody in the whole world listens as well as you do." Now, when I struggle to understand something he's explaining to me for the third or fourth time, I pray that somehow, someday, I'll be able to live up to my old reputation.

You asked if speaking is easier than listening. It does seem so, as long as I am simply trying to express something that is already set in my head, right in the front and ready to come out. I may get stuck on a few words and slow down to find them, but usually I can express myself pretty well. If I have to spontaneously put together complex ideas that are not already hitched up, however, then I struggle. So answering a question is hard. I'm wandering around in my brain trying to find information that seems to exist in pictures, metaphors, impulses, and feelings. And after I've found something relevant, I have to translate it into words. Usually there is not just one of these entities needing translation, but quite a few, all related in some way, and I have to figure out how to stitch them together. Often, I must admit, the "thought" that results is like a very badly knit sweater.

My reading is coming along. I do better with nonfiction step-by-step reading, probably because it doesn't involve so much processing of another person's metaphors and symbols. In novels, even the names are a challenge. I have to keep looking back to the charts I made to keep track of who's who. It's a little odd to realize that a name is a symbol for something that I have to recall and translate. I never used to get it, why some people couldn't remember names. Well, here I am now, unable to make any association with a name I just read a paragraph ago!

As for writing, I do find it easier than speaking when I am trying to convey lost or locked-up memories and experiences. I am actually surprised to read some of what I've written because it's almost as though I didn't consciously write it. I'll be responding to something you've said and suddenly there is this association, a sense memory that takes me to a place I've been but never talked about to anyone before, not even to myself. As my fingers put words to it, suddenly my experience takes shape in front of me on the screen, accurately describing something I didn't realize I could recall.

Last fall, I used to say to Michael and my mother, "Please remember this for me, because I know my memory isn't working and I don't ever want to forget this." Michael would say, "Some part of you will remember. Don't worry; you will." Now I'm happy to say that he was right. A part of me that I didn't even know was there was indeed remembering—not in a linear, verbal kind of way, but through images and sense memories.

As you said, perhaps now my brain is giving those images back to me in startling array.

Faith

4

Climbing

It's beautiful here. Michael and the children have gone to church, and I'm alone with the animals and gardens. All is peaceful. The blue heron has a lousy voice, but with looks as good as his and such a wing span, you don't need a sweet song. He's got a lot to say this morning; usually he's not so loquacious. I wonder what's up in the shiny green swamp. Everyone's singing this morning: happy frogs, crickets, birds, and now the splash of a chocolate Labrador in our pond, a puppy who is supposed to be at the construction site across the road. He belongs to the builder with the German accent, the one who arrives early, while all is still misty in the morning. He plays piano sonatas on his car stereo with the doors open, often waking me to the melodies. The dog is out of the pond now and rolling in clumps of just-mowed grass that smell so inviting.

I'm hoping that our chickens, Sunflower and Buttercup, will scoot back under the barnyard fence before the dog discovers them in the garden. "Wormy Butt" Buttercup seems to be healing well after a terrible incident with maggots. I don't think I've ever worked on anything so grotesque. Yet today she frolics happily on her breakfast date with Sunflower, no worse for the experience. I don't know if she's started laying again. We did find one very large and wrinkled egg a few days ago. I suspect that it's hers and that it will take some time and effort to get her laying back to normal. I can relate.

I'm relieved to be home this morning though I do feel a bit lonely, not being part of church for a year now. There's so much involved in going that I don't feel ready to take on. I could get there, but even if I was able to focus well enough on the service, the demands of spontaneous conversation would be excruciating. Barli was telling me that her autistic niece can't go to church because of the auditory integration required there, and that part of her therapy is to listen to the radio, where she has a little more control.

This week Lakshmi suggested that I try the same thing, except that I try conversing while the radio plays in the background. Yesterday I tried for about twenty minutes with Michael at breakfast and it just about drove me crazy. I'm also supposed to listen to stories aloud. At this point we've gone back to *Altar Music* again. It's familiar to me now, so I'm doing a little better with it. Eventually, says Lakshmi, I'll practice with books on tape, where I can systematically increase the competing background sounds—like listening outdoors—and then turn off the tape and see if I can summarize what I heard. This sounds impossible right now, but it will just take hard work, like learning to jump hurdles instead of only running around the track.

So anyway, I love you. And I'll respond when I can to your thoughtful observations.

Journal: Tuesday in September

Last night around midnight, our sick Ekta muttered to Michael, who was sleeping on the floor at her bedside, "Oh Daddy, I'm tired of being *so* tall. I don't want to have my head on the ceiling any more." What an insightful way to describe that out-of-body experience of a hotly fevered head, when most of you is hovering high above, looking down from someplace else. Bless her little heart, Ekta has been in this tremendously fevered state since Sunday evening. Finally this morning, her skin is starting to cool off, but she is still sleeping constantly.

Yesterday in one of those brief moments when her eyes opened and met mine before closing again, she said that she didn't want to be sleeping so much. I can certainly relate to that—not wanting to have to sleep any more. There were many months when I felt as if I was missing my whole life, and even when things got better I was still missing every afternoon. Unlike Ekta in her fevered sleeping, I had little awareness and never felt that hovering self, not that I can recall now anyway. I wonder if that "hovering self" belongs to a part of the brain that was injured.

I remember how peaceful my sleeping was at first, when the injury had removed my ability to analyze and reflect. Later, as I started to recover some cognitive abilities, I met frustration, disappointment, and anxiety in increasingly larger doses and the gentle sleeping days were long gone. I see now, ironically, how it was the very nature of my injury—stripping away my ability to reflect—that planted me firmly in the deep peace of the present moment. With part of my brain missing, there was no past or future begging for my concern. I wonder about people with other brain maladies, like Alzheimer's or cancer, and if there is something in the illness itself that eases fear and worry. I hope that as the disease progresses and removes one's ability to reflect, it brings its own kind of peace.

I am starting to think that healing is not the same thing as curing. Maybe healing does not mean becoming free of symptoms, or restoring to a previous state of being. It may mean something else entirely.

On the Sunday before Labor Day, our last day of summer vacation, Michael had the idea that the whole family should climb a mountain together. I hadn't climbed anything but the steps to my bedroom since last summer and I wasn't at all sure if I could manage it, but I wanted to try. The children were eager. We used to climb regularly, so I think the idea of a familiar family thing felt good to them.

We set out for Pinnacle. At the sign-in box there was a wonderful old stick that somebody had left there. It seemed to fit me perfectly and though I've never in my life used a walking stick of any sort, something about it beckoned, so I took it along.

Many times on the ascent, Benjamin said "I'm so tired; it's such a sleepy day. Wouldn't you rather be home, reading in bed?"

I said, "Yes, it is a sleepy day in the woods, and I'm so happy to be here, not home in bed." I was remembering last year, when I'd have given just about anything to be climbing mountains rather than sleeping those gorgeous days away. But I was very tired on the mountain and started leaning heavily on my stick. It had a nubby knot towards the top, smoothed and worn, just perfect for squeezing tightly as I pressed down hard into the root-bound, rocky trail and leveraged my body up one incline after another.

Many times I thanked the person who left this wonderful stick, as I realized that without it I'd never have made it up the trail. When we got to the first overlook, I sat down, exhausted but exuberant. A perky little chipmunk came out to see whether our group had any morsels for him. After tossing a few peanuts, Michael and the children were ready to press on toward the pinnacle. I said that I would wait there for them, but Benjamin protested. "Oh Mom, you're so close now! You've already come all this way. I know you can do it; it's even downhill for a ways before the last part to the top."

So I continued on with them, and when we reached the summit, we were the only people there. It was perfect: everything had looked misty and sleepy from the bottom but was bright green and clear above. I lay on a comfy rock ledge, eyes closed to the bright sun, while the children ate their sandwiches—supermarket specials that Michael buys only for mountain treks.

As I lay on those sun-warmed rocks, I thought about how I used to be so fit and athletic. The picture of me collapsed at the top with a walking stick in my hand was a little amusing, but Lakshmi always tells me, "Don't worry about what you need to do in order to get it right." I've had to work hard at that—not being embarrassed by my numerous strategies, like talking out loud to myself all the way through the grocery store. Sometimes it doesn't feel good to lean on whatever crutch I need at a particular time—although the mountain stick was one of my more glamorous substitutions for the-way-it-used-to-be. A perfect gift from someone I'll never know.

As we started down the mountain, Benjamin hung back with me. I was extremely slow and suggested that he needn't wait, but he said, "I like staying with you, Mom. That way I can make sure you're OK." When we met up with some serious-looking, heavy-duty mountaineers, Benjamin pointed to their hi-tech poles and asked the climbers what they were called. "Trekking poles," they said. Later, he told me that's what I had—a trekking pole, just like real mountain climbers use.

By the time we got to the sign-in box at the trailhead, I was so attached to my knobby wooden companion that I was reluctant to leave it behind, but I knew it would be a blessing to some other adventuring soul, just as it had been to me.

As we drove home I was thinking about last October and November, when I could barely manage to be out of bed for more than an hour at a time. I said to Michael back then that I didn't understand how a body could be so fatigued with all the sleeping I had been doing. It was nearly eighteen hours a day. Of course in those days we had no idea about the extent of my brain damage.

He told me then about the impact of inactivity, how bed rest alone can be debilitating. He related the study where athletes in top condition, I think football players, were put on total bed rest for several weeks. When they got up after that long period of inactivity, their physical stamina was tremendously limited. Later, I told my sister Barli about it and she said, "That's what happens to women who have to be on bed rest during pregnancy. They birth their babies, and then everybody expects them to be fine."

At that time it seemed as if I simply needed to increase my activity level slowly and eventually I'd return to my normal busy self. Looking back, though, I know that's not at all what was going on.

In late spring, after more neuropsych testing, Dr. Drudge shed some light on things. I began to understand that a healing brain consumes vast resources of energy to repair itself and rebuild healthy tissue. The many hours of sleep had been essential for that new growth. He also pointed out that when significant chunks of the brain are injured, all of the work has to be carried on with fewer channels in operation, and there just isn't enough "mental voltage." Thus the working brain tires quickly and frequent, prolonged rest is necessary.

Likewise, the brain needs fuel to rebuild, and so it finally makes sense to me that I developed a voracious appetite for sirloin steak, something my mostly-vegetarian palate previously would have repulsed.

Over these past few months, I've come to understand that a lot of rebuilding has to occur before rehabilitation can begin. All this makes me wonder about coma in a different way. It's kind of like there's a sign on the door that tells the outside world "Do not disturb! Major renovations going on here! We'll reopen when ready, not before."

In that case, the brain is anything but dead. Perhaps in coma, at least in the best circumstances, it is doing its most miraculous work, growing those incomprehensibly complex structures that it once grew *in utero* and must now try to reconstruct. A totally awesome endeavor that demands much patience and faith from those who are waiting on the other side of the door. I don't know that, of course; I just wonder.

Journal: Maine, September 14, 2000
Thursday afternoon on our balcony
at the Cliff House, Ogunquit

Michael and I are here for his dermatology conference. It is so gorgeous to be with the gulls and waves and rocky ledges that slice right down to the sea in perfectly-angled glacier-built steps. The air is deliciously salty and breezy, with clear blue sky and water that makes Michael's ocean eyes bright. I miss the children—their exuberance at the seaside and excitement over staying in a hotel—but it is comfortable just to be here alone with my husband. It feels a little lighter when there are no responsibilities for children.

We've just come in from a short climb on the cliffs. Since they're predicting rain for the next two days, we wanted to soak up the sunny splashing surf while we could. Coming up through the parking lot, we followed a woman in a neck brace. "Ooh, it hurts just to watch her," I said. I remembered when—months after I'd stopped wearing it—I came across my neck brace under the bedside table. I picked it up off the floor and instantly grew nauseous. Michael told me that often happens to cancer patients when they unexpectedly run into their oncologists months after chemotherapy, in the grocery store or some such place. The associations are that strong. I do recall the excruciating neck pain, head pain, and vomiting that preceded my "dark time," when I seemed to be asleep all the time.

Speaking of running into patients in a grocery store, that's something that became increasingly challenging for me. As I recovered to the point that I was out in public independently, I began to face the problem of being greeted by someone and not knowing whether she was just a friendly person I didn't know or someone I did know. And if I did know the person, how so? Who was she, and what should I say? It was one thing to receive letters from former clients and feel lost, but quite another thing to meet up in the bread section of the grocery store. There, we might say hello and pass our carts in three or four more aisles, while all the time I'm smiling and wondering if I know this person and finally, at the frozen waffles, I'd surrender: "I'm sorry to have to ask, but could you please tell me who you are?"

Once it was the mother of a former client. I remembered her after several prompts, and explained about my accident. The woman is a nurse who had cared for several head trauma patients; she took note of my color-coded store map and shopping inventory.

"Looks like you're getting great help from somebody," she said.

"Yes, my mother is a nurse and has been a miraculous help with this kind of stuff, and so are my husband and children." I said that just as Ekta returned with all the highlighted items from the frozen section and asked what we needed from "the next color."

That was one of the more gracious outcomes. Other encounters did not go so smoothly. Once, when Michael and I were entering a store, I started talking with a young woman I thought I knew well, but actually didn't know at all. I greeted her enthusiastically. Michael ushered me along gently and said, "You don't know that person; she's a patient of mine."

Oh well. Nobody ever told me this was another embarrassing part of recovery. It was clearly going to take some practice to get in and out of those situations more smoothly.

At least it felt slightly better than a couple months earlier when I received a letter from a client, a long letter about her life's journey and current circumstances. It hurt so much to realize that the person she thought she was talking to was not the person now reading her words. I had opened the letter at the mailbox, down the road. By the time I got back to the barn I'd made some sense of all the words, but I had to keep rereading to hold onto any meaning. And I tired so easily from the entire ordeal that I eventually sat down on a rock in the pond garden wall and cried. My old client was so tenderly pouring out the yearnings of her heart and here I sat, unable to grasp the letter's full meaning, unable to see her face or hear her voice among the echoes of my mind.

My mother was in the kitchen; I think she made me a cup of tea. Sometime later she told me about a conversation she'd had with a clerk at Neat Repeats, the clothing resale store. The woman asked her, "If I didn't know your daughter, how would I know that she'd had a brain injury?"

"You probably wouldn't," my mother replied. "It isn't something you see. If you started a conversation with her, you might become aware of her groping for words and losing her thoughts, and if you were interrupted she'd likely forget entirely what you were talking about or even that she was talking to you. But you might not notice any of those things. And if you didn't already know her and didn't have any expectations, you wouldn't necessarily notice anything not quite right."

Since then, for many months, I've wondered a lot: If somebody saw me now, how *would* she know? She probably wouldn't. That's one of the very frustrating and isolating aspects of this silent, invisible demon.

Journal: Friday morning, watching waves from our balcony

The moon was incredibly glorious last night. Round. Full like a pregnant woman's belly, she rose up from the sea and poured her sparkling essence out across the water. We stood there watching from a pay phone while Michael listened to Ekta recount the many details of her day. Suddenly a brilliant fiery-tailed meteor hurled itself out of the sky, plunging into the sea just below the moon.

We woke this morning to a soupy day, soft and gentle as gray velvet, the surf pulsing against gull-covered rock outcroppings and shooting its foamy white froth straight up like geysers. I'm not feeling particularly well, which is disappointing because I was looking forward to this little trip, a time to write, walk, think, but right now I don't feel too strong.

Journal: Saturday

A clear and sunny morning, just the kind of day you like to spend at the beach. Hopefully we will. Michael seems to be enjoying this conference and I'm enjoying this balcony—

room 523, at the end of the building, on what is actually the second story—with nothing between me and the sea except gulls. I am basking in the morning light while Michael attends a lecture on sun damage and skin cancer. His next is on "The Psychology of Appearance."

Neither of our children is interested in medicine as a career. Of course they're still too young to be enchanted with any adult work, but they both find the intrusion of on-call availability worse than inconvenient. Ekta says, "I'd never want to be a doctor. I have enough trouble just waking up in the morning; I certainly wouldn't want to get up in the middle of the night with people calling me all night long."

Michael wouldn't give it up for anything. I asked him recently if he still likes doctoring, and he responded unequivocally, "I can't imagine doing anything else. It's important to me to be needed—to feel like I'm making a difference to somebody. And I like to work hard. It's good for me." That's true about him.

I like to work hard, too. I'm starting to wonder if, and how, I'll do that again. I still need to sleep so much and go slowly. Yesterday it occurred to me that my brain had forty years of development prior to my injury and it would be reasonable to give it a few years to establish its new infrastructure. I've been thinking in terms of weeks and then months, but maybe I need to slow down my expectations—just stay with the healing and embrace the process patiently, with awe and a sense of creative discovery. Timing is so critical in every birthing.

But it is tricky to maintain my own rhythm. Because of its silent, invisible nature, my injured state is often unnoticed or forgotten by others. I talked with Lakshmi once about getting frustrated with people commenting how good I looked: "You look great! I'm glad you're doing so well." It is true that for a period of time I looked pretty awful—vacant tired eyes, gray-green complexion. I'd lost a lot of hair and my forehead was in a constant deep crease from the pain inside. I was thin and frail and moved awkwardly, holding onto walls or furniture to keep me anchored, balanced so I wouldn't tip over. When all that improved (thankfully it did), I guess I looked "all better." But when people would comment on it, I'd feel a terrible pressure inside, because I certainly wasn't "all better" and I didn't want people treating me as though I was. There was no way I could meet their expectations, or my own.

One of many wonderful things about Lakshmi is that she truly seems to understand what I'm talking about. Her empathy and affirming stories are so helpful. Like the one about the patient who, after several months of recovery from brain injury, told her he wanted to wrap a big bandage around his head so people's expectations would be more in line with his abilities. Or the stroke patient who had suffered both cognitive impairments and physical debilitation to one shoulder and arm. Physical therapy had improved things to the point where he no longer needed a sling for his arm. But he confessed to Lakshmi that he would still put it on when going out because people were more patient when he wore that visual reminder of his stroke. It was easier on his head to keep his arm in a sling.

Then she told me about her father's stroke and how her mother used to get annoyed with everybody telling her how great her husband looked; it left her isolated with her feelings. She got little support from people who saw his good looks as the sole indicator of restored health. Meanwhile, she struggled greatly to accompany him on an arduous, often disappointing, journey to recovery.

"Looks can be deceiving," Lakshmi said. She remembered her mother saying, "I'm glad he looks great. I wish looks were everything."

5

Singing Up a Rainbow

E-MAIL: TO CHRISTIN
DATE: SEPTEMBER 24, 2000

I was hoping to be able to write to you more consistently once my little ones were back on the school schedule. So far, it's been entirely too demanding. First Ekta was ill, and the beginning of the year always takes some adjusting. Both children have special academic needs and my attempts to coordinate these between two schools take a lot of intensive planning and meeting at the outset of the school year, but all should begin to settle within the next few weeks.

This morning, I was in the shower feeling weary and achy for the third day in a row. I was wishing things might be a little easier for my two academically, and thinking I don't have the energy to provide what they need right now. Then it occurred to me that they might actually be the first in their biological gene pools to become literate. If that's true, perhaps it's going to be a little harder and take longer than it does for those whose ancestors have been literate for generations.

I woke feeling rather discouraged and tired. So instead of hopping up in his usual get-going manner, Michael stayed in bed. Sometimes when I feel like this, it helps a lot just to have company. Then I don't feel so left out of life. Michael started talking about a nine year-old who is having a lot of trouble socially (lying, stealing, lacking empathy). The parents, loving and dedicated, are wondering what's wrong and how to help. We talked about how empathy is not something that can easily be taught. It requires a healthy, intact, active imagination—something this child seems to lack. Without imagination, both empathy and problem-solving become impossible and relationships can't happen. When I used to lead parenting classes, early childhood workshops, and playgroups, I tried to impress upon parents how vital it is to develop the imagination of young children, how it actually provides the cornerstones for emotional and cognitive competency. I don't know if most people understood. They liked the way I worked with kids because it seemed sweet, natural, and beautiful, but many missed the point of it, building the imagination.

I think about Laura Ruth, who taught Benjamin and Ekta for three years at the Waldorf pre-school. She always said that we need to offer young children beauty—that it's our job as their parents and teachers, out of our own love and joy, to fill them up with images of beauty. Upon that foundation, they will learn to think. The images should never be contrived but natural—a shell, a rock, rainbow silk dyed from plants, driftwood made smooth by water—and the child's mind will transform them imaginatively, building a foundation for later complex cognitive operations.

I wish every child could have a Laura Ruth in their pre-school and kindergarten days. What a different way of looking at nourishing the growing mind in order to raise great thinkers. All the academic and cognitive gymnastics we press upon children earlier and earlier may be robbing them of the essential beauty most needed to grow their young minds to greatness.

Considering my recovery from a developmental perspective, it makes sense to me now why beautiful, joyful, loving images were so healing. You wrote, "In my opinion, healing any part of ourselves begins with love and joy. The mind will travel farther and knit the body together more finely when it is enjoying the process. I think it is the artistic imagery and action that is most likely to heal you now."

I hope that with loving and wise intervention it's not too late for Michael's young patient. I suggested that perhaps having his own animal could be helpful. Relationships with animals are far less threatening than those with other nine year-olds. You can allow yourself to be vulnerable with animals, and they give so much to the senses and the heart. Maybe if he had the easier lover, his mind could knit together more joy, or its possibility.

Speaking of knitting reminds me of crocheting and your e-mail about teaching your red-headed niece to crochet—the cute girl you described as having stick-up ears like a mouse. Now that we have our fair share of mice moving into the barn for the winter, I've had ample opportunity to see what you mean about a mouse's ears, only I don't think they're quite so cute sticking up out of the grain barrel or Bravo's tack box. The other day Michael nearly stepped on one, and the poor thing was so terrified it ran for the first dark tunnel available—which happened to be Michael's pant leg.

In all my years with him, I've never heard the sounds coming out of his voice box that he made as he jumped faster and faster, shaking and kicking his leg wildly into the air. That mouse was traveling—rapidly—in the wrong direction, and Michael became a blur of yelping motion until finally the furry interloper came flying out into the air and scurried off. Now my mom tells Michael to rubber-band his pant legs before going out for evening chores.

E-MAIL: TO CHRISTIN
DATE: SEPTEMBER 25, 2000

Yesterday, we spent a rainy afternoon trying to tame the dragons in our basement. I wonder if other people's basements look as foreboding to them as ours does to us. We argue about what to save or toss and where to store things. Amazingly, yesterday was an unprecedented success, partly, I'm sure, because of my brain injury and how our life has changed in the last year. When you realize you've not needed something in over a year—haven't even thought about it—it's pretty easy to part with it. Although at one point Ekta surfaced from under a pile and triumphantly produced a single multicolored, extra-long shoelace with both ends so frayed that you couldn't possibly string it through a hole— not even if you were the heroine of the fairy tale and this was the last of your three trials.

"Now here is something really handy!" she exclaimed, and tucked it into her pocket. Michael and I rolled our eyes at each other and suppressed our laughter, amazed that for the first time in our deadly, avoid-the-basement-at-all-cost history, he and I found ourselves on the same team.

I do think it is a little funny that I might join my mother and Lakshmi as presenters at a conference on head injury later in October. The topic is something about "Strategies," which basically means being so ultra-organized, non-spontaneous, and compulsively neat that a programmed robot could function successfully in your place. This is so unlike the "old" me! Nothing could be a truer testimony than my chaotic basement. When my mother revamped our kitchen and living quarters to help with household routines and functions, the basement escaped her magic wand. It remains perhaps the last bastion of my former self's creative disorganization. Actually, my recipe box is also a relic. There are only a few real recipes in there, in the sense that a person could follow them and produce whatever the title at the top of the card suggests you might reasonably expect to enjoy eating.

Late last fall, perhaps in early December, I was walking with my friend Helen along the river by school. That was in the days when I didn't express a lot or easily. But I have a distinct memory of this one moment when I laughed till I cried. She asked me how the children were doing. This was long before we had any idea how extensive was the damage of my injury, and were still thinking that any day things would spontaneously return to normal.

I told Helen that Ekta was worried about me, and had been wondering when I would be a "real mama" again. She said she didn't like the way things were because she was afraid I might not get "all better." Benjamin said, "I'm not afraid of that, but I *am* getting tired of waiting so long. It's getting really inconvenient and *boring*." Then he continued—gently, as is his style, never wanting to injure—"No offense, Mom, but I'm getting really sick of lasagna. And when it's not lasagna, the only thing we have is scrambled eggs or chicken and rice casserole. I wonder if you could try something different."

Helpfully, he offered an idea. "When we were with Minnow, she made this really good dinner that maybe you could try. Hot dogs and beans. It tastes delicious. Do you think she could teach you how to make it?"

I don't remember what Helen said when I told her the story; most likely, she offered to bring dinner over that very night. I realize now that lasagna and chicken-rice casserole were the only dishes I had actual recipes for. And of course I had no sequential memory, so I would make a big pan of lasagna, then serve it for the next five days. The following week, I'd make another one—forgetting that I'd just barely gotten the pan washed and put away. No wonder Benjin was eager for me to learn the haute cuisine of hot dogs and beans.

E-MAIL: TO CHRISTIN
DATE: SEPTEMBER 27, 2000

I think I have told you, but maybe I haven't, how vital and incredibly healing our correspondence is to me. Your words and our conversation, as it grows in printed form, are opening up doors that my accident had bolted shut. And as the words materialize they are bringing back parts of me to myself. I didn't realize this at first, but I do now understand that our correspondence has helped immensely with my isolation. Not just the isolation I feel from the busy, productive, active world, but perhaps more importantly the isolation from myself—an isolation I experienced but didn't know or understand, as if there were a stranger living inside me, a really big stranger taking up most of the room in my little self. I remember I started to cry when your first e-mail response to mine began printing out of my computer in July. I was overwhelmed with relief, budding joy, and a sense of hope.

Once I thought that perhaps if I could offer anything to others out of this experience, it would be a worthwhile investment of my time to continue trying to remember, reflect, and write about it. But then I thought about how the brain is complex. Every injury is different, with its own pattern of rips, tears, and swelling. Furthermore, every brain is unique before injury—as different from every other brain as people's lives are different from each other. It's not like knees or stomachs, where we all have pretty much the same makeup working the same way, with more limited possibilities for fractures or malfunctions. And so I concluded that all my reflection and writing would serve only myself, nobody else, because every brain will have to do its own mending with its own stitches and we're likely not even using the same color thread or needle size.

I said that to Michael while we were in Maine. I told him that I didn't think I should keep on writing because, with this recent realization, it had begun to feel very self-serving. He disagreed with me. He said, "Christin's right. You have to keep writing down everything—as much as you can remember. Because if you do want to be helpful to anyone else, you'll have to offer it all. You never know what will resonate with somebody."

I've been thinking about what you wrote in that e-mail when you were encouraging me to print out everything, especially the part where you said, "This work you are doing is vital. You weren't sure you would be able to get the dance in your mind onto paper. But you are doing it! What you have written in describing what happens in your mind/brain as you sort out and link ideas with words is marvelously clear. Keep on."

Still, though, I'm considering whether I should do only a little bit of writing, just enough to keep in the practice of expressing myself. Like smallish homework assignments, but not paying so much attention to everything. What do you think?

E-mail: To Christin
Date: October 7, 2000

My dearest Christin,

So you think the "little homework assignment" type of writing won't work?

I like how you described what I'm doing: writing down

the essence; writing down the soul. "You can't do that in little assignments to organize your mind." I've never read that book you mentioned, but what you said makes sense to me, that "the healing part is in the act of writing that transfers from the 'homework' kind of writing to that kind that comes from somewhere else. Sometimes we have to write and write and write to reach that place."

Thank you also for freeing me to be self-indulgent in this process. I've reread that part of your letter over and over: "Please, dearest, don't just do this because it might be important for someone else. I'm happy that this thought got you started with the journaling, but you can let it go now. Do it because it will re-create you. Do it because it is worthwhile simply in itself. Do it because we love you, and we want you to love yourself as much as we do."

You said I must write everything I think and feel. And not worry about what will happen to this writing in the future. I'll try. Right now, I'm doing things in pieces. They don't feel too well put together, but I'll write whatever seems to be working its way to the surface of my mind and trust that somehow it will all fit.

The other day, the children were working on a new puzzle. They get these "top secret mysteries" in the mail every couple of months. And the first thing they have to do in solving the mystery is to put together a jigsaw puzzle so they can find out what the mystery is about. Once the puzzle is together, they can read about the case, meet the characters, get the "lay of the land" (every story happens in a different country), and figure out how to go about finding clues. Last week while they were putting the puzzle together they decided to try a new way of doing it. They started to work from the middle, because they wanted the added challenge of leaving the border till last.

That's how my recovery feels. Occasionally pieces fall into place, but there's no border or framework to guide me.

I've mentioned how my healing mind might mirror a child's growing mind in some important ways. There seem to be phases of development that are missing: in my case, missing because of the rips and holes; in the child's mind, missing because channels have not yet been created or matured. A few weeks ago, Barli was here with her family. I had a "petite epiphany" one morning when Ethan (her three year-old) and I were alone at the kitchen table. I didn't put it all together at the time, but I think I can now.

He wanted a straw for his lemonade bottle. We talked about how it would have to be a very long straw so it wouldn't get lost in the bottle. I pulled out a handful of straws from the drawer and placed them on the table where he sat. He told me he was going to find the longest one. Then he proceeded to pick up one straw at a time with his left hand and compared it to the one he was holding in his right hand. This worked well at first, but then he started to get confused over which straws he already had picked up and which he hadn't. At a certain point, he forgot whether he was comparing straws to the one in his left or right hand. He asked me to help him find the longest straw then. So I gathered all of them, evened up the bottoms on the table surface, and held the bundle while he chose the now-obvious longest one.

As I watched him struggle with the task, I saw myself and my own "mind ways." There are many tasks where the simple solution is not available to me. I go through a fairly complicated process, confuse myself with the steps I have to go through, and forget or misplace some data while I try to work with other information. All the while, what I'm trying to do is simple.

A few days after the straw episode, I tried to order pizza for dinner. We were three adults and five children. I used three different sheets of paper with lists, names, charts, and pizza pie graphs. I felt very pleased with my strategy as I dialed the pizza shop. Then I tried to relay the information I had so carefully prepared and what a fiasco! The pizza man was totally kind and patient, yet I had to start over several times. Finally, when I thought I had given the order accurately, he repeated it back to me and I couldn't make sense of it. So I said, "That's just right. I'll pick it up at six. Thank you."

When I walked in to pick up the order, the pizza baker said, "Looks like a big party tonight," gesturing to the pile—two feet high—of pizza boxes on the counter. It took me two trips to get it loaded.

I've never bought so much pizza in my life.

E-MAIL: TO CHRISTIN
DATE: OCTOBER 23, 2000

Good morning sweet Christin,

Great morning, actually. Totally brilliant. Frosty and clear. Everything aglow in bountiful sunshine. The thermometer says twenty-one degrees, and the weatherman says to look for fifty-five this afternoon. Most of the foliage is gone, yet the sunny yellows of the birches and poplars hang on, soon to be joined by the tamaracks (actually deciduous "evergreens") that produce the very last gold of autumn. The ripples across our pond and open areas in the wetlands are cobalt, perfectly matching the wings of my chubby bluebird friends. There are three of them, two males and one mama. It's a little unusual to see a trio; perhaps there was a delinquent son who'll remain in parental custody for the trip south. I worry that they may not return to us next spring because the field behind our meadow has been bought and the builder intends to start as soon as the ground thaws in March. Their septic system is engineered to exist right next to where the bluebird houses sit on our fence posts. Perhaps we can move the birdhouses and send out special invitations early, before the heavy-duty equipment arrives to scare them off.

I tried to photograph the birds this morning when they nestled into the yellow mum in my deck planter. What a picture—vibrant blue and yellow like in Van Gogh's sunflower paintings. I couldn't get close enough with my camera though, so I'll have to remember the image without a photo. I pray that we see them again next year.

In our yard, one oak (Michael's Fathers Day tree) still holds a few red-brown leaves and my Mothers Day birch flaunts her golden riches too. That's the tree where so many hummingbirds spend their summer. The rest are all bare. Only bird nests adorn their twiggy branches. Yet what sweet promise that picture holds—promise enough to carry us through the upcoming gray.

I was entirely delighted to experience the autumn time this year. Perhaps you know that I have an "October Journal." I may have mentioned it at one time or another over the years. It's a tiny journal I started a long time ago. I write only in the autumn. Of course last year I didn't write, and there have been other years with no words. This year I remembered and wrote. Here are a few pages:

October 8, 2000

Sunday afternoon with brilliant colors and misty, foggy clouds, the kind that drift along slowly, covering one mountain peak then another, raining gently here or there—always the possibility of a rainbow as tiny bits of sun peek through. How grateful I am to be awake this autumn time to see the leaves—not just to look at, but to walk in and smell, feeling rain and wind and hearing hundreds of geese. It has been one year since my riding accident and head injury.

Last year, I was asleep for most of this glorious show. The colors now seem exceptionally stunning, and the geese—calling from way above the clouds, invisible—are a mysterious crescendo as they approach, and then we hear the beating wings, millions of feathers making music out of the air. Music we won't hear again until next springtime, and then it sounds different—somehow happier than this bittersweet song of autumn, earth's last haunting lullaby before sinking into her dark and silent slumber.

Minnow is with her elderly friend Miss Lillian this evening. Miss Lillian said she wanted to come home to die. Friends are staying to care for her at bedside round the clock. Autumn seems like a good time to die, and she is ninety-three now. Last summer, for the Fourth of July parade, my parents drove Miss Lillian in their old VW, "Ladybug." Afterwards, she sat out on the Park House porch, and when the festivities had ended she tried to enter through a side door, fell, and broke her hip. The surgeries were not entirely successful; she was in the hospital for many, many weeks and eventually developed pneumonia, which earned her a trip to Dartmouth's intensive care.

Now she has said she wants to return to Gifford Hospice and die, because she's just too tired to fight it anymore. We're praying that her way will be gentle and she will feel very much loved every minute and not afraid. Hopefully, she will have a beautiful window so that she can see these brilliantly glorious hills in her homeland while she is strong enough to open her eyes. If not, perhaps she will see it in her dreams as Minnow and others share the beauty with her through their words and comforting presence.

It certainly is a most radiant autumn. I think if I were going to travel between the worlds I would choose this time as well. I love that song, "And he will raise you up on eagle's wings, bear you on the breath of dawn, make you to shine like the sun, and hold you in the palm of his hand." This is most surely a good season to fly, whether with eagles or geese or any other majestic winged ones.

Yesterday Michael, Ekta, and I went to the meadow up on Brownsville Road, the road past the falls where Benjamin and I were lost for hours the Easter afternoon of his first kindergarten year. He still doesn't know we were lost. He talks about it as our longest hike ever, in deep snow. I was scared, really scared. I kept singing songs and telling him stories, making up every game and adventure I could dream of to keep his little feet trudging along toward some hopeful sign of a trail (not visible when snow-covered) or a clearing that might mean a cabin or farmhouse.

We went back to that area yesterday with Ekta. Benjamin was at a sleepover at church, so it was just Ekta (and our dog, Brandy). We passed by the little creek where Ekta was overtaken by those nasty yellow jackets a few weeks ago. She snuggled in between the two of us there, but very soon recovered her spunky self and was off with Brandy, her bright red rain boots and yellow slicker completing the perfectly-colored portrait of an autumn walk in the rainy woods. We sang all the way to the meadow, three-part rounds, like "When autumn mists gather and leaves fall gently down, new strength in me rises to bear life's waiting crown." When we got to the meadow, Ekta and Brandy discovered a quail nestled under a cranberry bush by the old apple tree. I wonder what stories that tree must know, standing these many decades beside the old stone foundation.

The panorama was heavenly, with more colors than you would find in the most expensive collection of watercolor pencils, and they blazed brightly even in the mist and rain. We stood in the lush mountain meadow, green at our feet, while the hillsides in every direction rose up like flames around us. "Sing to these mountains and their beautiful trees," Ekta said, and she directed us in a harvest song she had learned at school. After many renditions and much laughter, Michael and I finally got it. Then the thunder started, distant rumbling over and over. "See," Ekta said, "they like your singing." Such applause I've never had.

It started really pouring on the way back to the car. But we kept up a good pace, marching to our three-part round once again, until Ekta stopped and said she was so tired she wished someone could just carry her. I said she was nine and too big, but Michael scooped her up, her limbs dangling this way and that, sticking out where they no longer tucked easily into the curves of his body. As I turned to look at them, my beloveds in the rain, I gasped, catching my breath. Through the trees right behind them a most gigantic, really bold rainbow was shining. It was so close it almost touched them. "See," Ekta said, "I *told* you they liked our singing!"

This morning, some out-of-town guests mentioned yesterday's rainbow. They said the cars on Route 108 were nearly crashing into each other, with tourists jumping out to photograph it.

"We saw it too," Michael said.

Ekta interrupted. "No, Dad; we *made* it." She explained, "I was teaching my mom and dad how to sing a new blessing."

A poem from a new Jewish prayer book by Marcia Falk says, "It is ours to praise the beauty of the world." Michael brought it home from church one day. I like it a lot:

It is ours to praise
the beauty of the world

even as we discern
the torn world.

For nothing is whole
that is not first rent

and out of the torn
we make whole again.

May we live with promise
in creation's lap,

redemption budding
in our hands.

A few weeks ago we climbed the Pinnacle, my first climb in more than a year, and I experienced anew that indescribable wonder of truly seeing things from a higher and wider perspective. It reminds me of Michael telling me, "Don't forget the big picture here." That was on a day when I was tearful over missing so much of my children's lives, just when they are growing so fast.

Last year I had only the first two weeks of September with them and then I lost the rest of the school year. I told Michael how detrimental I felt that was for them academically. He said, "There are things you never could have dreamed of helping them with before and now, because of your accident, you can offer them so much, can offer all of us so much."

And that was when he said, "Mountain climbing is good; it's helpful to view one's life from a distance." Now I am having a good day and I'm thinking yes, this has been a good year. I still have a long way to go, and at times I wish it weren't like this. But when I'm having a good day I can be grateful, or perhaps when I'm grateful I can have a good day.

Michael tells a story about a man who, regardless of what misfortune befell him, was grateful. In his way of thinking, the mishap always seemed to prevent a greater misfortune. He would say, for example, "It's a good thing our car broke down now, because otherwise we might be driving on that icy road and get in a terrible accident." I see some of that philosophy in Michael's attitude toward life. I'm not sure if it was learned in medical training or if it is simply his nature, but it's often good for him, and us.

Sometimes I do rue my ride that day; if only I had trusted my intuition. But my injury has given me a phenomenal experience. There are many gifts to be grateful for.

I remember when I first picked out my October journal, while living in Minneapolis in 1985. It felt on my cheek like the velvet of a horse's muzzle. At that time, a barn in Vermont with a horse of our own was just a dream. Today, as I write, our Bravo Beauty Boy is grazing beside the wildflower meadow and the blue heron weather vane atop the barn cupola turns gently in the breeze. In my dreams I'd never have imagined the joy, companionship, and healing that Ekta's birthday horse has brought me, or the pride, affection, and confidence Ekta has discovered with him. This surely is better than a dream come true.

As I read this October journal that spans many years, I realize that although I've struggled all year to discover and accept my new injured self, there is a core me, an essence that remains. I'm rediscovering its slow, slow awakening. The writing with Christin has been so helpful in that way: in our e-mails, I send my essence. Last month she wrote:

Who knows where that essence resides? Does it matter? The whole brain is, as you say, a mystery. Nobody knows. But that's what makes the work you are doing so very important. Not in a scientific way so much as in a humanistic way. You are reaching deep down and finding the core of your humanity. And your writing demonstrates how that is done. Your questions and your tears and your laughter and your struggles and patience and impatience all go together to create a map right to your essence.

Christin is always so reassuring and encouraging. "You are there, inside yourself," she told me. "The writing opens a door for you to see out, to come out, to play with us. To love us. That's all that matters. Keep it up."

Now, finally, I am beginning to feel some connection to the subjective experience of my life once again. Perhaps that just means I'm getting better adjusted to my new ways of being in the world: limited in many ways, yet expanded too—beautifully expanded through the changes and the long, long sleeping of my brain.

May Sarton wrote of trees and how, with the coming of autumn, they let go and reach for sleep and renewal. I feel, reading that, as if she describes me! There is much I can let go of, yet still my "self" remains. Earlier in my recovery I didn't understand that. It seemed I had lost my self, that she had just gone away. Now I wonder. Perhaps what I thought was my self actually isn't. Perhaps it's not a single wave, but an ocean.

I must sleep now, dear Christin. And I will sleep on these words: *Out of the torn we make whole again. For nothing is whole that is not first rent.*

6

Traffic Jam

E-MAIL: TO CHRISTIN
DATE: OCTOBER 25, 2000

I am so sorry to hear about your friend's teenaged grand-daughter. Thank God she's alive after such an accident! And thank you for telling me about her. Of course we will pray for her, pray that Tessa will wake up from her coma and discover life again.

There's another Tessa in our hearts as well, a child who lives in India. We found out about her through Heifer Project International. That's the organization working to end world hunger by providing farm animals to poor families, helping people create a livelihood that will nourish themselves and others in their villages. We first got involved with them after the kids turned their old playroom into a hotel and we started to have bed-and-breakfast guests. We were looking for charities to donate the money to, and Heifer Project was one the children chose. They have bought quite a lot of chickens and goats over the years, even a cow. We just read about Tessa in a recent newsletter. She received her goat a couple years ago. Last spring, the goat birthed two kids that Tessa sold;

she was able to purchase a gem cutter with the money. Now she has a dairy goat, a gem-cutting business, and an inspiring story to share.

I will hold that story in my heart as I hold your Tessa, praying that somehow, from the pain of this devastating accident, she and her family can create a hopeful future.

Being that you're into "nun stuff"—or at least have connections to people who are—I'm wondering if you know who did those nun studies, well-documented clinical studies of prayer and healing. They were conducted across all faiths, so it wasn't just Catholic nuns who did the praying, but also Buddhists, Hindus, and Jews. But I don't seem to find it in my head anymore. The only thing I come up with is that a patient who is being "held" in prayer does better than one who is not. I certainly had that experience last autumn. When one's mind is completely empty, and thinking is truly impossible, we experience another way of being in the world. Though the brain cannot contemplate (in a cognitive sense) the relationships that sustain us, we can feel their energies as truly as we feel the warmth of sunshine on our skin.

And speaking of holding people in prayer, I must update you on Miss Lillian, just so you aren't praying for the wrong thing. Her pneumonia didn't take her—in fact her lungs began to recover from it. And so she decided she would need to stop eating and drinking. But that didn't work either, because she started getting quite an appetite; she even asked my mother to bake her an apple pie! My mother's pie could win the blue ribbon at any county fair, and Miss Lillian polished it off nicely. Then she began to feel discouraged that it was taking so long to die. As one of her friends put it, "Miss Lillian and the Lord are having a bit of an argument." She added, "I think I know who's going to win."

Anyway, now Miss Lillian is eating and drinking and starting to walk, so if you are praying for her, it's probably best to know that. And there is actually quite a bit more I'd like to write about the many conversations I had with my mom during her caring for Miss Lillian and her fluctuating will to live. But I'll do that another time. Because I want to write about something else that your letter helped me to clarify. At least I think it did, but we'll see when I try to write about it.

You said that you think your own journaling tends to be boring and that it's difficult for you to describe what is actually in front of you—that somehow you may be hindered by reality. What I think is that you are hindered by the notion that you won't do it justice. If you are describing something that only exists in your imagination, there is no other picture to hold up against your writing to see if it looks "right" or as beautiful, or if it captures every nuance accurately, so that might seem easier than describing an actual scene.

But this is what happened as I read your letter. I loved the description of the tree out your window:

> It's an oak tree, all gnarled, with a gigantic hole in the trunk. I'd thought it was just an ordinary, large knothole, when I'd watch Eliot the kitten balance himself on its edge and peer down into it. I wondered why he didn't go inside. One day I went up to it and looked—well, it goes down and down and down. Empty to the point of invisibility. Now there's a topic for imagination! The lower branches of my office window oak are carpeted with velvety moss, a deep green that is almost black when dry, but that turns brilliant every time it rains. Lighter moss of a different variety hangs from the branches and puffs with the slightest moisture, turning spring green. It's fairy hair. Right now the orange-gold leaves and cinnamon-brown acorns are falling, covering the grass.

Reading the words, I come to know your oak with the forever hole and the fairy-hair moss that changes color in the rain. And I can smell cinnamon-brown acorns and see leaves falling to the grass. I don't really know what you're talking about when you say you can't do that very well and you're better at fiction. Then you included a description from my journal and said, "See how rich it is?" I read it and thought to myself, "That doesn't sound rich to me. It doesn't even begin to adequately capture the scene out my window as I sat on the couch looking out that afternoon."

And I was thinking about your oak tree and my foggy mountains as I walked back from the barn after feeding the animals this morning. I noticed that during the night the spider grandmothers had been very busily spinning among the naked twigs of our dwarf cherry tree. Still dew-covered, all those silken threads created a magical scene of dark red cherries and gray branches lit up with the spiders' garlands. I returned moments later with my camera, but as soon as I raised it to my eye, trying to frame a picture, the magic disappeared. Lower the camera, it was there. Raise the camera and close one eye, it no longer existed.

And as I came into the kitchen to heat up some tea water, I was thinking about the challenge of describing reality. If there is a picture that truly exists in real life, and we've seen that picture and really know it well, then if we try to create it again with words or film, our creation doesn't feel adequate. But if we don't have a real-life picture to compare it to, nothing real that we're holding it up against, the creation may be stunning.

This is why my journal description, to me, seems rather simple and inadequate, but you experience it as rich. And it is why your journal description to you seems boring, yet to me seems so nourishing. I know I've mentioned to you before how your lovely words and writings have nourished my imagination, fed my soul, and helped my mind to heal. To me your descriptions are anything *but* boring.

That was how all this puzzling stuff about the chasm between the way others see me and how I see myself finally fell into place. I realize that I'm the only one who has actually seen the whole, entire, real-life picture of my brain, mind, and soul. I've sat at the rim of my own knothole and peered, like your Eliot-kitty, into its vast possibility. Nobody else has ever seen the whole picture of my reality—as I haven't seen the whole entire reality of your oak tree, only the part you described to me.

As I have recovered certain faculties and abilities and am able to carry out particular functions (with many crutches and strategies in place), others experience that I am "fine." Like when it rains and the fairy hair moss turns brilliant green, it looks just right to me. But I don't know that the oak tree used to have six huge limbs reaching out from its trunk and now has only two because of lightning. I never saw the whole, entire, real picture of the tree. I don't know what kind of branches it has, now or ever. Only you know that, because you've actually seen it.

OK. So what's the big deal? What difference does it make and why does this matter? I know I've danced around this dilemma many times, puzzled and frustrated. This is such therapeutic work, trying to find thoughts and write about them. So the process is worthwhile, even if I can't succeed at conveying the meanings and messages I am grappling with. Now I'm starting to get myself very mixed up. I'll have to stop and go to bed.

But I do want to send this now, so you will know that we are all praying for your Tessa.

Christin dearest, my wise and loving friend,

Thank you for your understanding. It helps me greatly to hear what you get out of what I'm struggling to articulate, as I was getting myself very exhausted and confused with that other letter. And then you experienced it as "simply brilliant . . . a profound realization." You are so encouraging!

What a miracle that Tessa is waking up. Such joy for her parents even though, as you say, "no one really knows yet how far this awakening will progress . . . any fragile wisp of hope is met with ecstasy." Indeed!

The children come home early from school today. So I can't afford to tire myself this morning because I'll be with them this afternoon, getting ready for Halloween activities. Fortunately, their costumes are all set. Ekta is a most adorable tiger kitty cat and Benjamin is going to be a Dementor, like he was last year. Dementors are from the Harry Potter books. They are the guards for the prisoners of Azkaban. And the worst of all the punishments is the Dementor's kiss, which is worse than death because it means—uh-oh, I'll have to tell you later because I just forgot. It's really terrible, not something you'd want to remember.

We need to get pumpkins ready for the pumpkin walk through the woods tonight and make Halloween cookies for the party tomorrow. Ekta will want to take Bravo out for a romp too, and I'm hoping to be able to put a few things in the garden to bed for winter. So this will be a quick note.

I don't think I knew about your mother's brain injury and surgery. I only knew about her Alzheimer's. What you said about her was remarkable—exactly what I was trying to explain—especially the part about how she used to say "I have a hole in my brain." You said that she was aware of the missing part "only because she knew what her own completeness was, whereas we all saw the beauty she continued to be in the moment, and saw the part of her she presented to us, as we had always seen the part she presented to us. So to us the loss wasn't so evident." I really would like to know more about her brain injury and how you and she experienced her recovery.

You asked about my conversation notebook. It's a six-by-nine-inch three-ring binder with loose-leaf paper. A pocket on the inside cover holds my small calendar and daily folder, the file I depend on to keep track of today's tasks and errands. Most important, there's a pad of sticky notes clipped to the pocket, and two pens. My notes about conversations—both planning for them and writing down what is said—are written in designated sections. Divider tabs highlight the different topics and people: Lakshmi, rehab, kids' education, trips, household, etc. I add and delete tabs when necessary. Every couple weeks, I remove pages. Some I move to more permanent files; others I discard.

The notebook goes with me always, even to bed. It has to be with me at all times and I have a perfect bag for it—purple, with exotic embroidery and mirror work. It is unique and known everywhere as my bag, so it's not easily misplaced or forgotten.

And the last thing I wanted to tell you is that I am quite happy to be done with the head injury conference, though it was very interesting. People often mentioned humor as a critical factor in their recovery. There was one speaker who said he used to love reading but now, even twelve years after his injury, he doesn't read novels because it's too frustrating to track the characters and requires a lot of rereading. He told us that humor and religion pulled him through. He said, "It doesn't matter if you're not a religious person. Just find something higher than yourself that you can believe in— something important. It doesn't have to be a god; it can be your wife."

This e-mail feels like a badly wrinkled egg. So I'm going to turn off and head outside. Remember I love you. And also remember you don't have to respond with lengthy letters. I savor them, yet know you must attend to your book. And love to John too, and the deer.

Journal: Halloween morning

Ekta told me she lit two candles last night at the pumpkin walk. I wasn't there, as I still can't do night walks too well, especially not climbing through the forest. I missed it last year too, but I have vivid pictures in my mind from the many years I have been there. During the day, all the children in school carve pumpkins and carry them to their own chosen places in the woods. At night families return to a great bonfire and drumming circle, then walk silently through the magical forest lit up with the jack-o'-lanterns. At one place, there's an altar space with candles in jars for remembering people who have died.

So this morning when she said she lit candles for Tessa, the girl who's been so ill, I was surprised. "But Ekta, aren't those candles supposed to be for people who have died?"

"Oh, that doesn't matter, Mom," she said matter-of-factly. "Tessa needed a candle." Then she explained, "The lady gave me only one match because she said you're only supposed to light one candle. But I thought Tessa needed two, so I got a stick out of the woods, got some flame from the fire, and lit another one."

Benjamin just showed me the explanation about the dreaded "Dementor's kiss." It's in the third Harry Potter book, where Harry's teacher is describing how Dementors suck out the soul of their victims. Harry asks if the victim dies, and his teacher explains that it's far worse than death because even though the brain and heart still work, there's no memory and no sense of self. Once you have been "kissed," you are forever gone, merely existing as an empty shell.

Pretty awful. Guess that's why I forgot what it meant. Coincidental that Benjamin first explained it to me when he was trying to get me up to speed on the Halloween costume he was hoping I would make for him. That was last year, six weeks after my accident, and he was quoting from a fantasy about losing memory and self, ending up an empty shell. Imagine!

At the time, I felt like a costumed being myself, but I still believed that my real sense of self would return spontaneously. Very soon, I thought, this bad dream will end and I will wake up to my normal life once again. I had no idea what journey lay ahead.

E-MAIL: To CHRISTIN
DATE: NOVEMBER 9, 2000

First I have to say how much your story of your mama's brain injury meant to me. I love what you wrote: "Sometimes I thought that Mama's hole in her brain was a place for storing compassion. It was a place for feeling the pain of others, sort of a mind-womb. And there were those who wouldn't accept it because it frightened them. And there were others who benefited from it." Even though I can't quite pull it all together right now, there are many snippets of ponderings in my mind around her story. Especially the part where you said, "She always remained aware that she'd become different because of this experience, and she lacked the self-confidence that she previously had in abundance." That I can understand.

I have a total traffic jam-up in my head. Nothing's moving; all is totally paralyzed by the congestion. It's not a tidy traffic problem like backed-up highways into NYC or crossing the bridge into San Francisco. Those are predictable. Although you may sit for hours on end, you do know exactly where you'll end up. Everyone else is headed the same way and you'll all just inch along until eventually you arrive.

No, it's not that kind of congestion. My traffic jam is like those out of my childhood, in an Arabian marketplace or a city in India—the kind where the fruit wagons, camel carts, donkeys, pedestrians, bicycles, and boldly painted Mack trucks are all mixed in with big blue buses full of people hanging out the windows or riding on top, taxis, and other autos. All stuck, going nowhere. Everyone's pointed in different directions, beeping, shouting and waving; nobody can move. The hubbub comes to a standstill because there's so much chaos and congestion and not one inch of free space to maneuver into, so nobody can turn around, back up, or slide over. There is no real road to designate traffic flow.

That's how my head has felt for weeks now. I've not been able to muster enough mental energy to move any thoughts around. Things are stuck. I think it may be in response to excessive stimulation. Too many things to process and I just shut down. And of course there is the fatigue factor—I've needed so much sleep lately. When I drift in and out of sleep, I've been looking at the picture in my mind of those traffic jam-ups. At some point it occurred to me that if I could just make a little bit of room around some of that stuff, I might be able to think again and do more complex processing. So I started writing small notes in my journal. Now I am trying to write short bits about all the different things that have been stuck. Nothing is refined or developed.

The donkey cart isn't really on the right path yet and neither is anything else, but at least there is enough space so I can begin to find the appropriate path. The small bits probably won't relate to each other at all either, so this e-mail may make your head dizzy. That's a warning.

If, as Ekta says, we are "singing up that rainbow," well then, do we also sing up those terrible things that happen? I have a postcard that I've kept next to my toaster for about ten years. It has a quote from Chief Dhyani Ywahoo of the Green Mountain Cherokee. I read it every day. I've never quite grasped the concept, but I keep wondering about it. It says, "What occurs around you and within you reflects your own mind and shows you the dream you are weaving." On some level this seems quite true, yet it is sometimes hard to swallow.

The head injury conference was good, even though it was awfully tiring. One thing that was odd is that I realized I don't think of myself as a "survivor." To me, it doesn't seem like a title I've earned, because in my way of thinking that implies an injury much greater than mine, like flying off a motorcycle at a hundred miles per hour into a tree and being in a coma or a wheelchair. But the severity of a brain injury and the symptoms and impairments are not necessarily determined by whether you're ever unconscious or how long you're hospitalized, if at all. The truth is that I'm lucky even to be here. If I had not had my helmet or if I'd hit just slightly differently, I might be dead or paralyzed. By the grace of God alone, I am not.

I told Lakshmi three things that were especially good for me at the conference. For the first time since the injury, I realized that I can actually help others. For a long time now, I've felt like I am the one needing all the help. It's wonderful to realize that those professionals and caregivers at the conference thought I had something useful to offer.

The next thing that was great was the whole experience of "I'm not the only one." I know that in my head, but to see it and hear it and feel it in real life was terrific. Everyone was supportive, too. Instead of the brain-injured person being the one who makes all the accommodations, it was the others who accommodated us. I left my mother's side at one point and ventured toward the restroom on my own. I'd been there with her several times throughout the day so knew where I was headed, but I got a little disoriented and ended up knocking into one of the big display boards and it crashed to the floor. Immediately there were three people at my side offering assistance—so different from the usual stares and condemning looks that kind of incident draws in other environments.

And finally, the practice of getting organized and creating our talk was good hard work, emotionally charged, and a cognitive challenge. I'm going to send a few pages from the journaling I did while preparing my part of the presentation. After that I'll return to this traffic jam.

Journal: Before the conference

This morning I wrote a bunch of stuff for the conference, detailing the strategies that allow me to function effectively, but when I was done I felt like there was something missing, something BIG about the real work of recovery. So I added an additional page:

> To be compulsively neat and organized is so unlike the old me! Benjamin reminded me of that last week

when he said, "You know, Mom, one of the things that was really good about the way your brain used to work is that we didn't have to be so picked up around here. Like now I can't even leave a book on the counter for one minute. But before you fell off the horse we could put things wherever we wanted. We'd have piles of stuff all over the place, and you wouldn't notice for two months."

I feel sad about that, too—many times I do. The other evening I was in a dilemma over something that never would have mattered in the past, "getting my brain all frizzed up"—that's what my children called it. They both were trying to figure out how to remedy the situation and Ekta offered, "I think you should walk down to the barn, Mom. You can air out when you get down there."

Rehabilitation is a continuing challenge and can be hard, lonely work. Developing strategies and accommodations for living successfully with my "new brain" takes a great deal of getting used to and lots of patience. And that may be the easier part of recovery. Accepting who I am now and re-entering my old world with my new self is perhaps the harder journey. My capabilities are drastically reduced, and it's likely that I'll not recover to my former self. Yet I've come to understand that healing is not so much about returning to "life before brain injury." I have to believe that.

And I have to believe that the gift of brain injury and the grace of healing bring me to a new future—one that my old brain never could have imagined. I try to remain hopeful and accepting. In my more despairing moments, kind and reassuring words are close by, like Ekta's: "Don't worry, Mom. Just let the world keep turning."

So, dear Christin, that's what I wrote for my concluding remarks for the conference.

Then I had to time myself to know how long it would take to read my part. Standing alone by the couch with only the grandfather clock for an audience, I read my entire presentation out loud. But when I came to those ending paragraphs I couldn't get the words out. I was all choked up and had to stop.

Today I'm really mad at Michael for hollering at me this morning. He said that I need to be more organized. But I've become an expert at being organized! Nobody on earth could possibly be more organized about her morning routine and getting her children off to school than I have become. How dare he say that to me!

But the part that hurts most, I think, isn't what he said. It is that I don't really *want* to be so organized. Usually it doesn't bother me, but today I don't like that about myself— having to be so organized out of sheer necessity. It's how I survive, the only way I can function, but it's not "me."

So what's the big deal? You know, Vermont used to reside somewhere around the equator; it didn't used to have mountains or snow. Look what all the fracturing accomplished; see what beauty all the bumping and bashing about created out of this land mass. I don't hear these lovely green hills lamenting about how they used to be: all flat, hot and sunny, and covered with dinosaurs.

Dr. Drudge says the rank and file workforce generally does get back to work after a brain injury, but those with higher level professions often can't return. He mentioned that a dentist, doctor, attorney, or psychotherapist might not be able to return to work that requires a sophisticated level of cognitive functioning. He gave me good advice not to try to go back too soon and not to start vocational rehab too early, because I would not have the ability to resume what I hoped to resume, and it would be depleting and discouraging to spend my seriously limited energy and mental capability in a lesser capacity. "First things first," he said. "Start with successful functioning in your home and with your children. You have to set your priorities, because you won't be capable of doing everything you once did."

Sometimes when I see my neighbor Gretchen driving to work I think, *Why not me? I'd like to get back to work.* Then it is good to remind myself that I am back to work in a way, because I am back to mothering. Gretchen is not a mother (not yet, but please God let her be in this lifetime). And I am grateful for my motherhood and homemaking work.

I'll write more once I manage to get a few more camel carts and overcrowded buses moved out of this heap. In the meantime, dear one, I'm loving you, hoping the deer are safe in your yard, and wondering (along with the rest of the country) who will be president. Many birthday hugs, lovely Christin.

E-MAIL: TO CHRISTIN
DATE: NOVEMBER 11, 2000

We have just come in from the barn. It's getting dark soooo early. The animals come in all on their own and they'd be asleep for the night at five o'clock if we didn't go down, turn on the lights, chase mice, and close up the doors. They sleep an awful lot in the winter. They rally to greet us, and it's a lovely comforting feeling to be tucked into the cozy barn all together.

On the way back to our kitchen, Ekta sniffed the air and told me, "Smells like the rain will be stopping soon—probably tomorrow, Mom." It was a gentle rain, the kind that leaves tiny droplets on blades of still-green grass, just enough water to catch the moonlight and turn the meadow into a carpet of glistening jewels.

Inside, I was happy to discover your letters on the computer. And no, you had not told me about the effects of illness on your mama's brain and functioning. But it made sense to me as soon as I read it:

> I remember that Mama's ability to "keep on top of things" suffered even if she had an infection like a cold. I think I told you this, but maybe not. It seemed to me that her brain had to refocus its energies to healing the infection in her body, therefore she lost some of her other abilities for a time. Emotions did it also—the same thing. A powerful emotion took up so much energy that it would exhaust her.

Feeling relieved and hopeful, I said right out loud, "Oh yes, of course!" I've been fighting this cold for several weeks—sore throat and sinus involvement too. Maybe the traffic jam isn't so impossible; I'll just wait until my brain takes care of these nasty bugs. Then I'm sure I'll be able to summon the mental energy needed for other things. Thank you so much for that insight.

Journal: Saturday morning

We just finished shoveling two piles of manure and bedding, Ekta and I. We're alone this foggy gray morning. She told me the good thing about turning over the compost piles is that it reminds us of really hot days.

"See," she said, holding up a clump of steamy hay, "it's nice to feel the heat and think of summer, don't you agree?" I certainly do.

Perhaps later today we'll walk through the dying fields and collect butterfly cocoons from milkweed stalks and leafless bushes. We can bring them home to our wildflower meadow, where they'll sleep through all the blizzards. And in the springtime what lovely wings we'll see.

I'm thinking today about accurate diagnosis for health problems—how it's so important but can be really evasive. Sometimes it takes more than one type of specialist and several different avenues of inquiry. It's like looking for cocoons. You don't know where you'll find one, how long it will take, and whether it will hatch.

How lucky that we stumbled upon Dr. Musiek, the audiologist. His evaluations were extremely enlightening. I'm not able to recall any of it now—enough to write about it—but I am hopeful that he will be able to help both of us, Benjamin and me. Benjin is clearly diagnosed with central auditory processing disorder, and we will return in January to begin training for his remediation. I have to go back in a couple weeks for more testing. I'm going to be a research subject. The doctor said my results were fascinating.

That's not exactly a comfort. I remember when Michael was in residency, he said he hoped never to be an intriguing case for any physician. But at least if Dr. Musiek is intrigued, he will be using his diagnostic tools and expertise to further our understanding of what is going on with my auditory capabilities. And he does think that a lot can be accomplished through retraining. That's hopeful.

Acceptance

7

Snowed In

E-mail: To Christin
Date: January 15, 2001

It seems like a very long time since I've written anything at all. I did manage to piece together our family's annual letter, which took ever so long, as you might imagine. But I am happy to say it's finally in the mail, and of course there is no evidence of my many frustrated efforts—the crossed-out, scribbled pages, or a stamp across the top margin that says DRAFT #201. But if I think about it, I barely managed a paragraph for our holiday letter last year; Michael did the rest. So that's progress.

The snow is falling like crazy this winter—every day since the first flakes in late November. It's like we're in a Hollywood set for the movies. No awful blizzards or freezing rain, just plenty of snow, light and fluffy, constantly floating down around us. My gardens are fast asleep. But this morning, the stone bunny who sits amidst lilies in summer has just one long ear poking up out of the drifts, like a periscope checking on the world out there. That's kind of how I feel too, emerging from beneath a deep snow. And I promised myself that I would be very careful.

Though I am eager, I must start slowly. So I'm going to

send this much only, not much more than hello. And always, I love you.

Journal: Monday before Valentine's Day 2001

Good heavens. I can't believe my last time on these pages was not long after Halloween! But reflecting now, it does make sense. November is when I came down with that awful sinus thing and was totally out of commission for many weeks. I felt lucky that it was my sinuses and not post-traumatic scarring, with headaches that can onset a year or more after head injury. At least with sinus infection, you know that eventually it will clear. In my case, it took about six weeks and two different regimens of antibiotic treatment. What a setback to feel so depleted. The general state of my overall health was so weakened that this just wiped me out.

November also was when I had the first MRI of my head. Right after my accident, I had a CAT scan that did not show anything abnormal, but I didn't have the MRI then. So getting those results was a mixed blessing. On the one hand it's probably better to know as much of the story as we can know, but on the other hand it's a bit shocking to find out very concretely, with tangible evidence, that part of your brain is shrunk and shriveled. *Post-traumatic left occipital and posterior parietal areas of focal atrophy.* That's how the radiologist's report described some of the damage.

November was when Benjin and I began our appointments at Dartmouth with Dr. Musiek; the assessments and his evaluations were so insightful. Then we moved swiftly into Advent and Christmas activities, New Year's, Benjin's birthday, Michael's birthday, his mother's visit, and now—finally—I'm able to take a deep breath, or I should say catch my breath.

In January, finally and officially, I moved out of my counseling office at Threshold, with all the logistical and emotional challenges I had hoped to avoid. I decided not to renew my license and professional insurance, and the others had long since painted over my shingle on the sign with somebody else's name. But that's a story for another day.

So here I sit, cozy on the couch with the two fuzzy snowman pillows I made for fireside winter stories. The sun is streaming through the children's folded paper stars, making the window look like a cathedral's stained glass. I'm writing in the shade of three huge geranium pots that are sitting on the sill. Their fuchsia and coral blossoms are brilliant, holding their color even as they dry up and pass on toward seeds. They, like everything else around here, seem to have found a way to manage in spite of my completely unpredictable care.

There are many piles all over this house—in every room's corners and on shelves and available floor space. I am starting now, just barely, to have the cognitive capacity and physical stamina to begin—very slowly—the sifting, sorting, unraveling, and piecing together of these misplaced and tangled papers that have accumulated for a year and a half. Now when I sort through the stuff it feels like I'm piecing together my own life—not somebody else's. That's great progress!

Yesterday I discovered a bright lady beetle among the dusty piles. I brought her down to the schefflera plant that happens to be covered with aphids that I'd really like to get rid of. Just a couple days ago when I discovered that problem, I was wishing for a ladybug or two, along with the summer weather that usually accompanies them.

Mostly I do like winter. Just these past few days of heavy snowfall, ice, and severe, minus-fifty windchill have been a bit much. My body wants to shed that winter stance (chin tucked down, shoulders hunched up against the cold) and my skin longs to be really hot and bare. So I'm happy we just made a deposit on a weeklong trip to Punta Cana in the Dominican Republic. This summer will be our twentieth wedding anniversary, the one when we're supposed to take the dreamed-about honeymoon we never had. When we married, we honeymooned on our graduate student budget—a weekend trip to Canada—and promised ourselves a Hawaii-type fantasy trip on our twentieth anniversary. So here we are. We'd rather not go away in the summertime, so we'll fly on April 21, the date we got engaged (in an airport, when I was racing to catch the plane back to school in England).

One of the things about this head injury that troubles me is the type of person I've become because my capabilities are not steady or reliable. Since I never really know how I'm going to be, I'm hesitant to put myself in situations that are unfamiliar, with the potential to demand more from me than I'm capable of. I can't count on myself to pull through, and others can't count on me either. I *really* don't like that. I was always the sort of person who wasn't afraid to say yes. I had plenty of confidence in myself. Now I'm hesitant to leave home.

Helen recently told me about a family whose house burned to the ground when the dad, who is recovering from a head injury, tried to make his breakfast. Everyone got out safely, but their home is gone. I can't imagine how impossible recovery would seem if my entire house burned down. Nothing familiar to remind me who I am, no safe haven where I can begin to feel some sense of efficacy and mastery in my environment. No quiet upstairs corner where my bed waits for me, a pile of pillows ready to refurbish my overwhelmed neural pathways at any time of day. And the ticking of the grandfather clock, a sentry posted at the couch where I spend countless hours doing the work that I hope will help my brain heal and learn.

I really understand why elderly people like to stay in their own places. The sense of competence is much greater there, where everything is familiar. And when one is too feeble to engage in life in a busy way, it is nourishing to be surrounded by old memories—the stories held by so many objects and photographs—and to be warmed by the energy ensouled in their rooms. I've become like an elderly person.

I must say I have some reservations about our choice of Punta Cana as our honeymoon destination. It's nothing but all-inclusive resorts. No real towns, which doesn't suit my sense of social justice. The native people will be in the service jobs, trying to eke out a living on pitiful wages. The differences between skin color and economic status will be striking. That's not exactly the experience I would choose for my children. Yet it is one reality—an all-too-pervasive reality—that they'll have to grapple with.

On Martin Luther King's birthday Ekta said to me, "Mom, I just don't get it." I was looking for something in the refrigerator while she and Benjin were sitting down to dinner.

"What, Ekta? What don't you get?" I asked, fully expecting the usual dinnertime litany of complaints about her unfavorite classmate's mean behavior, or perhaps something like "I don't get why we have to eat carrots again."

So I was taken by surprise when she said, "I just don't get it, why some people think white skin is better and why they're mean to people who have skin like mine."

"Because they're stupid," Benjamin said immediately.

"But it doesn't make any sense," she said. "How can

somebody be better or worse because they have white skin or dark skin?"

"You're right," I told her. "It doesn't make any sense at all. People aren't good or bad because of their skin color."

"But Mom," she protested, "some white people think that. They did really awful things to the black people."

We talked for a while. I explained about Reverend King, his great love and faith. And how he fought peacefully, without killing people. But Ekta wanted to know *why* the white people were mean to the black people. I felt so inadequate— me in my white skin, trying to explain to my dark-skinned daughter the inexplicable ugliness of humankind. But I had to try.

"In our house we say everybody can have their own ideas. You don't have to think what Benjin thinks; you can have your own opinions and he can have his. We believe that people can disagree and be different, yet still love each other and get along. But not everybody agrees with that. Some people say, 'You have to believe what I believe, live the way I do, look like me, and think like me. If you're different, you're bad.' Some people feel threatened by others who are different, and so they are mean. Sometimes they do terrible, cruel things."

"Is that why they made all the black people into slaves?" she asked.

Benjamin joined the conversation again. "It wasn't only dark-skinned people who were slaves. Remember Moses and the Jews in Egypt. They were white but they believed in a different god, so Pharaoh wanted to get rid of them." He talked about slavery and the Civil War, Hitler and the Holocaust. He told her that Martin Luther King got a lot of his good ideas from Gandhi, who liberated people in India from oppressive British rule. But it still didn't make sense to Ekta, why some people are mean to others because of the color of their skin.

Benjamin grew a little impatient. "No offense, Ekta, but you can't change history. It's done, so what's the point of this conversation anyway?"

Ekta was quiet the rest of the meal. After everyone had left the table, she still sat there in the candlelight while I cleaned up in the kitchen and Benjin went upstairs.

After a while she said, "God must feel really disappointed about the way things turned out. I'm sure he tried his best when he made those people. He didn't mean to make cruel people. I don't blame God; it's not his fault. It's just things didn't turn out right."

I put some carrot sticks back in a bag and sealed it up. "I bet you're right, honey. I'm sure God feels very sad about the way some people are."

E-MAIL: TO CHRISTIN
DATE: FEBRUARY 15, 2001

Good morning dear Christin,

Here it is already one month since I thought I could start writing again, slowly—but I didn't think *that* slowly.

My garden bunny is totally buried again under many feet of snow. In fact probably something like five feet, I would guess, because usually, in that same garden, two copper-green hummingbirds "sing" from a wind chime which hangs next to the forsythia, just about five feet up in the air. Now the pipes of the chime are silent, and only the wing tips and beaks of the birds are visible through the drifts. Skating on the pond, we are surrounded by snow banks taller than Michael. We have to crawl up the bank and slide down onto the ice when we want to skate. It looks like a beaver slide—

you know the way they build those muddy shoots down to the river bank when they're logging upstream.

Anyway that's how it is here—totally snowed in—and that's how my writing feels too. As you know, I am trying to be careful, and there have been many other things I've had to give my limited energy and mental space to. Writing is just not something I can do when I'm tired. There are an increasing number of organizational tasks I can do when my mind starts to wilt, though. I'm now able to fold and sort laundry even when I'm not firing on all cylinders. And I can sometimes get groceries put into the proper places on a tired brain. Those are good indicators of progress. One thing I like about not writing for so long is that since I am not paying close attention to my course of recovery on a daily or weekly basis, I am pleasantly surprised when I start writing and realize that I can do something new.

The last time I wrote in my journal was right before I broke down in November. On Monday this week, when I began writing in my journal, I realized that I was recalling and recording a conversation I'd had with the children on Martin Luther King's birthday. That's a pretty significant step when you consider that I must record most conversations of any length or depth as they are occurring in order to process them and be able to recall them later. This makes me see that there is progress, though I don't always realize it day to day.

The agate turtle you sent is with me every night, sleeping between my layered pillows. As you said, her pace is grace-filled and her ways are wise. She helps me remember the wisdom of going slowly.

I am looking forward to the winter break that begins next week; both children really need a rest. People who never had learning challenges don't quite get it—how arduous and taxing, how unimaginably exhausting, the classroom learning experience can be for children whose minds work differently from what school is set up for.

Part of my remediation, and Benjamin's too, with Dr. Musiek is something we call Read and Sketch. (It has a technical name, but that's what we call it.) We choose a passage that conveys many ideas and read through it, one short segment at a time. After grasping the main idea for the segment, we have 45 seconds to render that idea in a small pencil sketch. Then we move on to the next segment and sketch that. These steps are repeated until we have created a page with about ten or fifteen little sketches. Then we try to recall and retell the entire story (or information, if it's non-fiction) from our sketches. This is retraining my brain to absorb verbal information—which I have trouble processing analytically—by converting it into drawings, which the brain processes in a more gestalt ("big picture") manner. The steps are reversed in the retelling phase of the exercise, when the brain must convert the pictures back into the verbal analytic. The merits are obvious. It's also very good for a child like Benjamin, who has auditory processing and memory difficulties. The goal is to lighten the load on the weaker verbal/analytic part of his brain by training and strengthening his ability to construct gestalt representations to process and store information.

I was looking at your e-mail dated July 16, 2000. I had told you that in order to grasp a story such as your novel, I would have to turn it all into diagrams and flow charts in my mind, and you said this makes you wonder what narrative is, what it depends upon. You wrote, "We must have a part of our minds dedicated to historical flow. I know that children don't seem to have this until they are a certain age. They can listen to stories but cannot tell stories that have any narrative flow."

Yes, clearly with my ability to sequence events hindered I was unable to grasp the flow of your novel and keep things in a meaningful order. I think I was aware of it then. But the thing that I am only now beginning to understand is how much narrative depends on our ability to continually convert words into pictures and back again. To do that requires well-developed analytic and gestalt capabilities and a great network of pathways, allowing rapid, fluid communication between them. After my accident, my analytic functioning was very much impaired while my gestalt processing was as strong as ever. In fact it seemed even stronger, but Dr. Musiek explains that it seemed so intense because of my lack of analytic capability.

In the July 16 e-mail you continued, "Recently I've been thinking of how difficult it is to actually tell a story. We have stories in our minds, but to give them that flow, to actually turn them into narrative, is a difficult craft." Yes indeed.

You concluded by asking, "Am I getting too philosophical?" My answer at that time, seven months ago, was a loud YES. It was impossible for me to follow your train of thought. Not today. Perhaps it's my turn to ask you: am I getting too philosophical? And that makes me smile. Yet I do wonder if my rambling efforts to convey something that has become clearer in my own head may be coming out muddier than ever.

I need to rest now, but I wanted you to know I am thinking so much of you, and I'm hoping your novel is being well-received!

Happy Sunday to you sweet Christin,

My little crowd headed off to church this sunny cold morning. Having been up since five o'clock myself, I'm about ready to return to bed now, but wanted to write first. The house is very cold. I think that when the temperature is below zero outside it feels even colder inside, although the thermostat remains constant—sixty-two during the day, fifty-five at night. The windows behind my computer screen face to the north, so no sunny warmth shines in here. I'm typing in my woolen fingerless gloves, the ones I used to use for springtime gardening when it was really too cold for that type of work but I was eager to greet the plants—even weeds! More recently, though, they have been my autumn barn gloves, thus are filled with the scents of Bravo and Naisa. Funny to smell them here at the computer.

I'm hoping you are well and wondering if you still have canaries. Hard for me to believe you see them so early in the year. Around here they are definitely a welcome herald of spring— in May, if we're lucky. Right now, we're delighted just to have a chickadee or two. Recently we had a couple. It is always a surprise to see any birds in winter, other than those huge noisy crows that hang out all season.

Recently I was thinking about the role of loneliness in illness and recovery. As one disappears from the world and others' lives move forward, I find that I am very much alone. All is still and very silent. There is a deep intimacy with one's self that develops out of this much aloneness, because most of what usually distracts us is stripped away. A certain wisdom and peace come with the solitude. I can be grateful for that on this silent wintry morning.

8

Moving Out

Journal: Sunday morning, March 11, 2001

I'm feeling eager for the time when a warm breeze and birdsong will blow through my bedroom window along with the morning light! Last Sunday, after much chopping, I completely cleared the deck of snow and ice. The temperature was above freezing, with the slightest hint of thaw in the air. We sat outside for hours. Michael read *The Hobbit* to the children while I dreamed up new yard and garden plans; we'd just returned from the flower show and my head was full of ideas. The sun was glorious! I was happy to have that day. I reminded the children of how when they were little they loved when I cleared off the big deck in the spring. They would bring out their toys and trikes and play all day outside as if it were summer, even though we'd be surrounded by high snowbanks all around. I even got a little sunburn on my cheeks that Sunday, but days later we were once again covered with several feet of snow.

The animals are getting restless for spring, too. Bravo especially wants to romp and race the wind whenever it blows, but there's hardly much room for maneuvering. Yesterday Benjin helped me clear out the doorways around the stalls and gates. We have to use the blower now because the banks are much too high for me to shovel up and over. I'm hoping that's the last major snow removal we'll have to undertake this month; soon it's supposed to start shrinking instead of piling up!

The animals seemed happy to have a bit more walking space around the barn, but Naisa, the crazy goat, decided to venture too far. She managed to walk along crusted snowdrifts for a time before hitting a treacherously deep, un-crusted soft spot—and sank down almost out of sight. Fortunately, we were home, and I heard her bleating desperately. The children ran to her aid as quickly as they could negotiate the hard crust and soft spots.

Today I'm in bed with (I think) pneumonia—or maybe it only feels like pneumonia because my body lacks the strength to overcome what might otherwise feel simply like the bad cold it probably is. I had hoped to take the children to the mountain today, but that's out of the question now. Instead, I'm looking at the mountain from my bedside windows. The couch beneath those windows is stacked with piles needing attention. Only two bags of leftover papers from my office remain to be sorted and put away. It will be a relief to finish that task and close a chapter that has been left painfully open-ended for too long.

E-MAIL: TO CHRISTIN
DATE: APRIL 8, 2001

Good morning lovely Christin,

The others are off to church without me, as I greatly need some down time. I've been thinking of you often, sending sentences in my head, so now I'll try to get some of them into the computer.

Yesterday I was at the barn in the early morning. There is so much snow trying to melt around its base, it's soon to be afloat. I was trying to coax water toward the drainage pipes by chiseling paths through the ice-crusted banks when Michael came home from his office. His car window was wide open to this first tease of spring air and sunshine, so I heard the radio as he turned into the barn drive and stopped the engine. The commentator was interviewing an author, a woman who wrote the story of Seabiscuit, a true account about the horse, his jockey, and their comeback together from a tragically disabling accident.

Michael handed me a hot latte and we listened together to the rest of the interview. The story of the horse and jockey, and the author—who revealed her own disability with chronic fatigue/immune deficiency syndrome—touched me. She said her fatigue was so debilitating there were days when she couldn't get out of bed and wondered how she could go on living, but always this book was there for her. She could lose herself in the lives of Seabiscuit and his jockey and the struggles of their recovery. They never ceased to inspire her.

It occurred to me this morning that perhaps the reason I am not writing my "story" any more is that I'm really tired of myself. I feel stuck in my recovery and my life; it's best not to give that too much attention. By the grace of God, my experience is neither sensational nor tragic; there was no coma, no miraculous recovery defying medical explanation. I am thankful beyond measure for all of that! I acknowledge how tedious my experience is. I would rather lose myself in somebody else's story. And perhaps I got wet feet or cold feet, or whatever you say. Around here, we're both wet and cold.

I haven't written anything lately. I've been trying to do the things that are on my lists each day, while staying ahead of the laundry, kids' homework, mail, bills, grocery shopping, and also doing whatever I can to avoid sinking into dark spaces where I feel badly stuck. In my way of thinking, this piece of my life has been the most trying—not just mentally but spiritually, though it's not a lofty spirituality. Rather, this has been a mundane discipline of cultivating hope. I have to climb out of despair on a daily basis and try to court acceptance. That's pretty ordinary stuff, really. To a certain extent everybody has to do it at some time or other in life.

We had thunder last night, a lovely sound we've not heard for many months, and enough rain that now the tips of the fence posts are poking out of the snowy meadow, neatly outlining its perimeter every ten feet. Yet our snow-banks remain impossibly high and we are still walking down a steep bank to get in the house. What a happy day will dawn when we once again set foot on grass and climb four steps up to our front porch. Of all years to have our tropical island "honeymoon," this is surely the best—the longest winter to cut short by hopping on a plane. Two weeks from today, we will have our feet on hot sand.

I'm still nervous, but not thinking too much about it. Just looking forward to sun and warmth. There's a lot to do, so I need to focus pretty diligently. This afternoon we will build a small ramp so we can transport Bravo in our van to Burlington. He is going to a large boarding and training facility for a month. Ekta and I will go over regularly before we leave for our trip and again when we return. Hopefully he will learn a few basics so Ekta can train him to drive this summer. Once he learns, he can be hitched up to anything. I wonder if you know that mini horses are now being trained as guide animals for blind people. Naisa and the chickens will stay here in the barn with Gretchen to look after them. And Brandy will be home too. She is such an old dog now, she couldn't possibly go anywhere, but Gretchen and Peter and their dog and cat are good company so I hope she does OK.

We've already received our passports and tickets (including four coupons for Imodium). Now I'm trying to find sunglasses and sandals for the children, whose feet have grown bigger than mine while wearing snow boots these past six months! We drive to Montreal on the twentieth and fly to Punta Cana the next day. I'm taking that beautiful journal you sent me at Christmas and I've got an embroidered bag necklace for the agate turtle. So you will be there too, in spirit, on the palm tree beach. I hope you are well and that your stories are singing easily from your heart.

Journal: April 10, 2001

I bought food for Easter this morning. A whole bunch of pansy flats were for sale and many of us stopped to admire their perky purple faces, but nobody took any home. "Where could you put them?" one lady asked, gesturing with a flick of her wrist toward our snowy surroundings.

"On your dining room table?" I responded, and she smiled. I would buy some and plant them on my table if we weren't leaving next week for Punta Cana. We just had a call from the travel agent, who said that Quebec City is hosting some sort of World Summit talks the weekend we're due to fly out of Montreal. We're being forewarned to expect long delays at the border crossing. Evidently they're anticipating thousands of protesters.

I wonder what they'll be protesting. I marvel at people who put so much energy into causes. It must feel like terribly important work to them. It probably is, but I just don't know any more. An odd thing about my injury and how I experience life now is this feeling I have that if anything matters then everything matters, otherwise nothing does. It's one of those existential ponderings I drift off into when my mind can't quite focus on the business, or should I say the busyness, of life. Does any of it matter?

In the past month we've had more snow than we get in some entire winters. I didn't believe it could happen this late, but here we are. I'm desperate for spring now. The children have cut neat little stairs in the snowbank at our front porch; at least the days have warmed enough to soften the snow so they could do that. We still have to walk down to get in our front door, which we usually ascend to from ground level. Ah well, Easter will come, and so will the grass.

At least the chickens have started laying, a hopeful sign. Ordinarily they won't set foot in any snow. Yesterday they all strutted out of the barn yard on a thin ribbon of gravel that the noontime sun had drawn out of the surrounding snow cover. My neighbor called to say they were parading down the mud-and-puddle road—very inviting for my worm-searching hens, who were spotted passing the mailboxes. They seemed so pleased with their great escape I was reluctant to herd them home, but eventually I brought them back to the barn. I even managed to find the teeniest shoots of grass, bright green blades that my shovel uncovered as I was clearing out manure on the south side of the barn.

Little by little we're making our way into mud season. The mourning doves returned yesterday to my Mothers Day birch tree and the food Michael leaves for them on the railing. Five geese came back, too, honking overhead. But after circling over the frozen water they left again. They prefer open water to land; I don't know where they'll find it. The wetlands are starting to show that gray-silver color that suggests they are mushy, not icy. I wonder if the geese can land in it.

Seems as though the song of the peepers will be still a long time coming, but who knows? Perhaps when we return from Punta Cana, Benjin will sleep with earplugs again. The Easter Bunny usually brings him a new set in his basket, along with the chocolate eggs and vegetable seed packs. He loves the silence of winter and is always perturbed by those inconsiderate frogs who party all night in April and May.

I've started setting out our clothes for Punta Cana in neat piles on the bedroom couch, beside the grocery sacks of papers from my former office. It would be nice to return home and not have to see them sitting there on the couch, a reminder that there is no place for that part of me.

The day Michael helped me clear out the office was gray and gloomy. I was happy for his company, his strength, and his efficiency, but mostly for his patience and the way he respectfully handled all my stuff. That's all it is—just "stuff," quite ordinary stuff, really. But it was immensely important once upon a time. I was grateful that Michael was not in a big rush. He seemed willing to give me the time I needed to collect the bits and pieces of myself and remove them from my office.

I don't have an office now. There isn't a place "out there" in the world where I do my work. I still don't know yet if I'll ever do that work again—it's too early to answer that question. But I've certainly reflected often on that notion this past year, wondering when will be the right time to contact Vocational Rehab and see about my profession. Whenever I get close to thinking "maybe next week I could make an appointment," something always seems to happen that overwhelms me.

I'm remembering also what Dr. Drudge said, that often after brain injury people have some level of fatigue that continues forever, and so recovery also has to be about learning how to manage your energy and activities very carefully. I can't "do it all" anymore, so what are my priorities? They have to be self-care, mothering my children, and managing our household—in that order. Everything has to be planned around those commitments and what I can manage.

When I think about returning to work it always used to mean returning to my office, clients, and many meetings. It meant giving that well-educated and professionally-experienced part of me to the busy world out there, where people engage in important things that matter. That's what I believed. I certainly didn't neglect my home life. My children always were my first priority and greatest work—it's just that I wasn't limited to my home. I did it all; now I can't.

At a recent medical appointment, the nurse ran down a checklist of questions: Do you use caffeine? Alcohol? Drugs? What's your level of stress? Do you work?

That last one stumped me. "Do you work?" I said to myself out loud. Then I repeated it, like I've learned to do when my brain doesn't seem to be registering input and producing a response. I was staring at my hands, folded on my lap, and trying to come up with an answer. "Do I work?" I said again out loud.

The nurse said, "Homemaker counts. You can say 'homemaker' if you want. That could be your work."

I kept staring at my hands. And slowly I said, "No." Then I got the rest of the words out. "No, I don't work. Not since my accident. I have not been able to return to my profession."

I watched her writing my words into the chart. We talked a little more, and she told me she's diabetic and can't have children. I didn't follow it all very well. But the part about not having children stuck. After she left the room, I was thinking how lucky I am to have my children.

Then I thought, "I do work. I just don't have a profession anymore. In fact, I do have a profession, but I'm not working in it right now." I didn't want to say I'm a home-maker because that might imply that I don't have any other profession, and I wasn't ready to believe that about myself.

A few weeks ago, when I was in a pretty desperate frame of mind, quite depressed about being stuck and dependent, Michael and I had a bad conversation. After things between us went from worse to beyond-worse, he cut it off in exasperation.

"What's the point in this conversation?" he asked. "How can I even talk to a person who can't remember what I just said and gets it all mixed up?"

It's true. Meaningful dialogue is rather impossible at that point. I certainly was struggling to make sense out of his words and my thoughts and hold it all together. He tried to tell me that he feels unappreciated and like I am expecting him to do everything I can't do. And don't I have any idea how busy he is?

I tried to tell him that I'd give just about anything to have some of his "busy-ness." That my uneventful stay-at-home nothingness is not of my choosing. "And I hope you never ever in your lifetime have to learn how hard this is. How much it takes to spend yet another day on the couch while everyone you know goes off to their day of people, activities, and causes they believe are important and feel satis-fied to participate in."

It occurred to me that weekend after the fight that per-haps, if it were just me, all alone— if I didn't have a husband, kids, house, barn, animals—if I just left all that and took my-self to a little one-room apartment, someplace warm where I could walk to my job and to a small grocery market, then I could probably take care of myself. I wouldn't be dependent on Michael to provide for me financially and I wouldn't need to rely on him to "fill in" for me in this life we have built together that I can no longer participate in the way I once did. And I could have a real job—something small but manageable. It would be absolutely wonderful not to feel so utterly dependent, and I could probably have some sort of satisfying professional work.

Feeling so desperately dependent on a husband (or anyone) was never a place I wanted to be. Thinking about it made me wonder if it was a mistake not to pursue a lawsuit after my injury. I used to think it was a bad idea. Once I started to have a somewhat working mind and a little energy, it didn't seem like a worthy pursuit to spend it on. Even though, according to the attorney, I would likely get some sort of settlement, what good could possibly come out of it? None, I thought. Besides, I didn't feel like suing anybody. That's not the kind of person I am. Michael agreed with me. He said often with patients he sees that the process of having to prove disability seems to contribute to further disability. It seemed far more helpful to focus on all the things I *could* do and how well things were going, rather than invest my energy in trying to make things look as bleak and debilitating as possible. I always said that was a great gift of Michael's profession, that we didn't have to rely on my income, and I could be taken care of financially without having to sue anybody. I still believe all of that. It's just that when I feel really stuck I start to wonder.

I still haven't answered the questions that Lakshmi gave me (in October, I think) about my work. They're actually hard questions to figure out, and I've been trying to determine what exactly keeps me from being able to do my work. I think at first I expected that answer to be fairly simple and that once it was uncovered I'd be able to fix it (or somehow accommodate it) and then return to my office. But the more I paid attention, the more I realized it was not simple, and eventually I came to acknowledge that it was time to move out of Threshold.

I decided to do it at the new year, after relinquishing my license. I called to schedule a time when Michael and I could clear out. One of the therapists called back and asked that I wait about six weeks so they could replace my furniture, curtains, and paintings a little at a time. This would allow them and their clients to gradually get used to the change. I was offended, horribly, but didn't immediately know why. My mother also was indignant. She continued loading the dishwasher but said, "It's not as though they haven't known. Your stuff has been there without you for well over a year. They took your name off the sign and rented your space out to someone else. People you don't know are using your things. And now they want you to give them six weeks to redecorate?"

I went upstairs and drew water for a bath. When Michael came up an hour later, I was crying. "I figured out why this hurts so much," I told him. "First, she doesn't seem to have any idea what it takes emotionally for me to come to this point. She seems oblivious to my sadness and my struggle to accept an outcome I would not have chosen. But even worse, it feels like they want me to disappear unnoticed—gradually, so the transition is not so apparent.

"It hurts a lot to leave that place," I continued, "and I want somebody to notice I'm gone. I don't want to just disappear for their convenience." At the same time, I admitted that I'm ashamed of those feelings.

"That's human. It's nothing to be ashamed of," Michael comforted. "We all want to be noticed. People want to leave their mark on the world somehow. We want to be remembered after we're gone. No one wants to be forgotten."

"But it's not like I'm dying," I said. He was silent, and I went on. "Well, I guess part of me has. I guess that's what this must be about. I don't want to be told, 'Hey, could you postpone the burial for six weeks to give us a little time to redecorate, so it won't be so shocking?'"

Later that evening I called back and spoke to the message machine. I said I'd be coming in three weeks to collect my furniture, pictures, plants, and other things.

Michael and I got it all loaded. I left my keys, closed up, and we headed home. I was doing fine—so far so good—until we got home and unloaded everything from the van into the guest room. We just brought the stuff in and plopped it down there. Then I sank into Gram's pink velvet swivel rocker, leaned my head against the crocheted Irish lace, and sobbed.

Later, Michael took me to lunch at Trapp's. We arrived back home to find a dozen glorious pale yellow roses from Helen and Brendan. The card simply said, "We love you." And it was perfect, just perfect.

I called to say thank you. "How could you have known?" I asked. She said Michael told her I was moving out today, "and I just wanted to honor the passage."

What a gift it is to be understood. So affirming not to be judged or told, "You shouldn't feel that way. What's the big deal anyhow?!" Lord knows I tell myself that often enough. What a gift it is simply to be understood.

Slowly, over many weeks, I've found places for my office stuff, and there are just two grocery sacks left. It will be good to empty them now. And I'm not feeling like I need to leave my family or my home and beloveds and run away to a real job—at least not now.

The snow is melting. There are rivulets through the farm fields, and last year's cattails standing straight up look like so many masts on sailing ships, waiting to be rigged for great adventures.

Journal: Tuesday in April, after Tax Day 2001

The thaw is coming. This morning I woke before dawn to birdsong. Not the full-bodied chorus of summer, just a petite ensemble with enough variety to assure me that many of our winged beloveds have arrived.

A few days ago, upon returning from school, I went to the kitchen to start dinner and Benjamin went out on the deck "to see if spring is coming." Heaved greatly by frost and burdened far too long with many feet of snow, our deck now appears to have more in common with a roller coaster track than with anything pictured in out-door living magazines. After a few moments, the door opened and Benjin called in, "Hey Mom, the geese have landed! They're back!" with as much enthusiasm as if he was announcing that his favorite hockey team had won the Stanley Cup championship. Delighted, I went out to join him on the deck. Sure enough, a small flock had landed on the icy mush over by Lawrence Brook, honk-ing exuberantly. We stood together for a moment. I'm not sure which made me happier, the return of the geese or my twelve year-old son's joyful reverence at the event.

He went back inside for binoculars and was soon call-ing for help. I pulled them out of Aunt Marrion's sewing cabinet by the door. It still functions as a sewing cabinet, with all her thread on wooden spools, but it seems the best place to keep the binoculars so they're handy in a hurry. I handed Benjamin the black case and returned to my pot on the stove. He remained outside for awhile and then came in to the couch and sat down.

"Did you get a good look?" I asked.

"No, they're really hard to see. They must be awfully far away." I wondered if he might need a new prescription for his glasses; I'd seen them easily, even without binoculars. Then he burst out laughing.

"Oh my gosh!" he said, looking at the thick black caps still fixed over the lenses. Pulling them off, he headed for the door, muttering, "OK, now let's try this again."

At that moment I thought about Christin's letter, and how precious her gentle perspective is. She totally reframes things, like removing the lens covers so now I am able to see something quite different. Our doubts and insecurities surely can be seriously blinding! Reading her response was like lifting a huge weight off my shoulders. "Honey, you are an artist," she wrote.

> There are a few wonderful books that fit the genre that I think is yours. May Sarton's journals fit this genre. You say your life is boring, but what did she do? Tend her flowers. Go to the post office. Write to her friends. Mourn the loss of a beloved. Tame a cat. But the words she used to tell about these "boring" events simply crack open the boring shell of human experience and release the soul! This is your talent as well. You make your life there in Vermont live and shine in your words. . . . Keep your journal. Write about your days, your children, your animals, your work at recovery. When you are on that warm beach next week, write about being on the warm beach. Write with a love for writing and a love for the object of your writing. And just keep doing it, a bit of it every week. Don't worry about the outcome. Just live, PJ. Just live—and write that life. Your words will be heard, my beautiful girl. Your words will be heard.

Now I actually *want* to start writing again, although I still feel more exhausted than ever.

Gratitude

9

Honeymoon

Journal: Thursday before Punta Cana

Our bluebirds are home! They just flew into Benjin's birdhouse by the "four sisters" fir trees. How lucky we are that spring has been so long delayed and the construction vehicles aren't here yet. I don't imagine the ground will be ready for digging any time soon, so maybe we're in luck as far as bluebirds go! I called our builder last night about coming over to check on our rockin' and rollin' deck. He asked how I was and I told him I was fine, now that our bluebirds have arrived. He noted, "That's pretty good assurance that spring will happen."

"Yup," I agreed, "as long as they don't get discouraged by the lack of green and disappear to a sunnier destination."

He said the deck would likely settle down in time, once the frost gets out of the ground, but that he'd be over soon to check it out just the same. He told me he'd just come from a place where the frost had heaved up one corner of a woman's home. She'd put in a new atrium and now her big picture window was crooked. "She was quite a little upset about that, but I told her there's nothing you can do except be patient. Wait for things to settle down." That's good advice for most dilemmas, I suspect.

In three days we'll be in Punta Cana. Today will be busy, since we head for Montreal tomorrow and must finish everything this afternoon. Thankfully, Michael is off. He'll take me to Burlington so I can bring Bravo's harness to his trainer and we'll try him with the bit. Ekta also wants me to drop off the special box she's prepared, in case he loses his first baby tooth while we're away. I remember her birthday party, when she opened that box, a gift from Lizzie. One of the other girls said, "Too bad, there's nothing in it. What will you do with an empty box?"

Lizzie smiled and shrugged. "Put things in it."

"Special treasures," Ekta agreed. "Thanks, Lizzie. It's perfect."

She told me yesterday that I should send Lizzie a note to tell her that the box is going to be for Bravo's first baby tooth. "Tell her it's a perfect box for special things."

I'll have to add that to my "to do" list, which is already much longer than I can handle in a day. Hopefully Michael will manage the shopping errands.

Many more geese are honking, and I've got to run off now. First stop is the tanning booth, which I've never visited before in my life. But a travel tip from someplace suggested utilizing one for a few days before your trip so you don't burn up in the Caribbean rays. It sounded like a good idea, given my extremely pale complexion.

The sunbathing in the Dominican Republic is European style, with women topless, and that part of me certainly hasn't seen the sun lately. Benjin is aghast at the thought. He assumed we were joking. And when we insisted on the truth of it, he asked incredulously, "Mom, you're not *really* going to do that, are you?"

"If I didn't, I might be the only one with a top on," I replied, "and wouldn't that make me look pretty odd?"

"Oh gosh," he said. "If that's really true, then I'll be getting well-acquainted with the interior of the hotel."

Journal: Thursday night, late

A flooded basement was not on my "to do" list, but that's what I returned to after the tanning session. Our visit to Bravo and the shopping mall was postponed by a greater need to visit the hardware rental for a sump pump. How lucky that Michael discovered it first thing today, instead of tomorrow on our way to Montreal. Imagine the mess if we'd not discovered it until our return from Punta Cana—oh my goodness. In any event, the rental pump worked nicely and a contractor arrived late morning to replace the faulty one. It had not been properly pumping to the pond and had caused a terrific backup of ground water all around the footings. All is working properly now and we did manage to accomplish most of our shopping errands locally.

We'll plan to visit Bravo tomorrow on our way to the airport. That way we can make sure the trainer has his harness while we're away, so her leathersmith can alter it if necessary. And we'll see how he takes to the bit, too. We need to bring another bag of carrots and of course the special box for his tooth.

I have just lit a candle for Barli, who called to say she's in early labor. She said they'd be burning the candle I sent for Nicko's birth. They still have a few hours left on that one because they had to blow it out when it almost caught the midwife's hair aflame. Barli's hoping to have her wee one this evening and avoid the long, lonely, nighttime laboring. I told her I'd be up and sending lots of energy. She said she needs courage, too. I promised to hold her in loving arms and send all the courage I've got. Now I'd better get the packing finished.

Journal: Punta Cana, Tuesday afternoon

I am sitting in the late afternoon sun, up on our balcony. I've never been in the top of a coconut tree before. It's lovely up here, with the palm fronds all glimmering from the coastal rain shower that's just poured over them. Our room is on the top floor, so we're at the same level as the coconuts, hanging out together in the Caribbean sky. My skin is warm and sun-drenched after a day at the beach. Vermont's snowy ground seems impossibly far away.

A couple days before we left, I dressed Ekta in clothes pulled out of the dryer. She exclaimed gleefully at the sensual pleasure of hot long johns against her legs and asked, "Is this how our skin will feel in Punta Cana?" And it does feel like that. So far, everything has been simply perfect, and I've been counting my blessings every minute.

This beach has to be just about the most beautiful seacoast on earth. Its natural character has been well preserved by the resorts; the only developments here are eco-sensitive hotels that have done a great job of retaining the coconut groves and gardens. Such a delightful honeymoon to have for our twentieth anniversary, and what fun to share it with the children. Ekta plans to come here for her honeymoon, too. When she told me that yesterday, she added that I could come with her.

We've had a whole week on this island, floating in time and space, so far away from our usual lives. The only phone call was this morning, when Michael called to request the porter. The Dominican people have been friendly and helpful beyond our expectations. Ekta says God's smile is the sun and God has a really big smile here. So do the Dominican people.

E-MAIL: TO CHRISTIN
DATE: MAY 4, 2001

Hello Christin dearest,

I'm writing to you with the window wide open behind my computer monitor and a breeze sucking the blue-dyed raw silk curtain up tight against the screen. It's a warm breeze, about eighty-one degrees, I think, and feels rather like being right back in Punta Cana. I was so happy to return to no snow. And while the first couple days seemed unbearably cold and gloomy, we've now plunged right into August weather, hot and hazy. Though it will most likely change very soon, for now my spirits are soaring with the warm wind. And while Benjamin coughs at the manure smell it carries, I delight in the tractors returning to their fields and the promise of crops soon to sprout.

Punta Cana was marvelous, more marvelous than I ever could have imagined. And we had a totally fabulous week. The only disappointment was that it had to end. I'll write more about that later, but first I must tell you how perfectly uplifting your letter was—the one I received just before leaving for our trip. I had been in such a funk (as you may have gathered) and your words were so liberating and encouraging: "Crack open the boring shell of human experience and release the soul."

Thank you a million times! You really helped me to see something that I was quite unable to grasp in my tedious endurance of recovery—that the everyday things do make up a life, and they matter. I love May Sartons's journals, too. I read them a very long time ago and saved them in my grandfather's glass bookcase, the one where he kept his sea-shell collection with specimens from his travels. I only put my very most favorite books there. My writing is certainly a far cry from Sarton's, but I see your point: that if I simply live, and write that life, my writing will be about far more than my injury. As you put it, the injury is only a secondary thing, "a wash of color" over my life. Anyway, it never works to worry about the outcome of writing; it only works to love doing it.

I got out Sarton's *The House by the Sea* and realized that she was living and writing in the very town in Maine where we go to the seacoast every year, York. We discovered it by accident one day when the children were tiny, shortly after we moved to Vermont, and we've gone back every year since. The first year, Benjamin stood on tiptoes in his Mickey Mouse sandals outside Goldenrod's candy shop. For hours he watched machines toil away, stretching salt water taffy. I didn't know about York when I read *The House by the Sea* long ago. Now someday I'll have to reread her journal.

Your response was affirming, and truly helped me to embrace my life again with a bit of interest and a sense of blessing—not to mention how much better it made me feel about writing. And as my spirit lifted somewhat I also was able to contemplate my physical being and lack of vigor a little more compassionately. Rather than assuming that I was making myself sickly and weak through a lack of activity, and then trying to force myself into impossible situations, I began to listen more gently to my tired self.

My intolerance of the cold had increased to the extent that I could no longer even walk outside. And I had become so exhausted I was unable to consider initiating anything that might actually help to improve my depressed state. Now that's a bad cycle to get stuck in. Eventually I decided to do something about my fatigue, hair falling out, and a big lump in my throat. It turned out to be a thyroid problem. I had the blood tests and ultrasound and found out that, for whatever reason, my immune system had shut down my thyroid and my metabolism was all off. The disorder is not something that will go away, yet it is easily and effectively treatable.

You might imagine how happy I was to discover that there is a simple way to alleviate at least some of my fatigue. And with this new understanding of my condition, many things fell into place. My lack of vigor was not the result of a lethargic, discouraged ambivalence about life, but rather a natural response to my body's struggling metabolism. And my cold intolerance had not grown out of a winter spent lazily lamenting on the couch. I was tremendously relieved and somehow liberated by the diagnosis—even though it does seem odd to be happy about a disorder!

That happened soon after receiving your e-mail and just before we left on our trip, and all seemed much better rather quickly. It will take a while to correct my hormone level and I'm not writing volumes just yet, but my outlook is greatly improved. It was wonderful that I got both your e-mail and the thyroid diagnosis before leaving on our trip, because I was able to rest more happily and the entire vacation was quite perfect. I wanted to say thank you for that.

I'm hoping you are well. And how is your springtime? You seem quite ahead of us; perhaps you're moving closer to summer already. I remain ever grateful for your words and your love.

E-MAIL: TO CHRISTIN
DATE: MAY 5, 2001

Hello sweet Christin,

I must be a real country girl. For me, even Burlington, Vermont is too much city. I'll be happy when Bravo comes home from there. Our little country horse has had a few "big city" challenges of his own, like adjusting to pavement after our grass and dirt roads here. He refused to walk on the "real road" for several days, and when he finally did step out onto it he froze at the sight of the bright yellow painted lines. We had quite a time convincing him it wasn't a gigantic snake or worse. And if truth be told, I'm not sure all these paved roads aren't a rather poisonous specimen of snake coiling round our planet.

For our vacation I wanted to go somewhere totally undeveloped, naturally quiet, and beautiful. It turned out that our Dominican destination was extremely rural—no roads, highways, or cities. Nothing was there, really, except the tiny thatch-roofed airport and the resort. I hope Punta Cana can stay rural for awhile, but as soon as the roads get built, things are sure to change. And who am I to say the people there shouldn't enjoy all the conveniences we in more "progressed" places have come to rely on?

Benjamin is in Boston with his Unitarian church class for the weekend. In preparation for the trip he did a small project on Henry David Thoreau. It was interesting to browse Thoreau's ideas regarding humanity, nature, development, and life in general. Though written long ago, *Walden* certainly has relevance for today, especially regarding our notions of progress and how best to live.

What a treasure that you have a letter from May Sarton saying that your book *WomanChrist* fed her soul each night as she went to bed! Yes, it is disappointing to keep the letter tucked away in the dark file, but essential to preserve it that way. Could you possibly have it copied and then frame the copy for your desk or wall or wherever you'd like her words close by? You could get several copies, so that when one fades you'd just slip in a new one. That way you could enjoy her words and the sun all together.

Some people pull massive shades across the windows whenever the afternoon sun shines brightly, sealing their entire living room against the light. It seems a little crazy to me to live your life without sun just so your couch pillows won't fade, but I guess some people worry about those things. I rather like the look of well-sunned pillows—kind of like well-worn wood floors or thinning elbows in a favorite sweater. But that's me. Anyway, I'd surely keep May's letter in the dark too, but also find a way to have her words close by.

Michael saves things in books. He's forever sticking mementos of this or that between the pages of his fat books: a note from one of the children, a letter from a patient, or a quote scribbled on the church bulletin, slipped between the pages of Shakespeare, Sherlock Holmes, or Mark Twain. When he does it, I say, "You'll never find it again." But he always does—not when he's looking, but at other times—and it's always a surprise, still a treasure, and generally totally relevant to the moment.

How fortunate you are to have gladiolas. I've only done them once, because around here they have to be dug out and wintered-over indoors. I've never been that organized a gardener. Maybe when I'm old I'll grow gladiolas, really bold ones. My great-grandmother did; she had a special bowl for their blossoms. When Grandma died, my mother gave me that bowl, and right now it's filled with the roses I dried from Ekta's birthday. She turned ten this year—my baby.

The night of her birthday, we were walking back from the barn under a starry sky and she said she doesn't want to have any more birthdays. She said she doesn't want to grow older because "that makes you grow older too, Mom, and I don't want you to die. I don't ever want you to leave me." She thought that maybe we could stop all of that just by not having any more birthdays.

I told her it doesn't work that way but that even when I die, "I'll still be with you. I'm never going to leave you, Ekta. My bones may grow too old to hold me up on this earth and my body will die and I'll move on to the star world, but even then I'll still be with you, loving you, always near."

"Not near like you are right now."

"That's true. You won't feel my hand in yours, but I'll be very close."

"Will I hear you and see you?"

"I think so," I said, wondering to myself how that actually works. "I think you'll see me when you need to."

"Should I look for you in the things you loved here, like in flowers and mountains and sunshine?"

"Yes," I said, "that's where I'll be. And I'll be in your heart too, forever. I promise."

My forsythia is in bloom! Brilliant yellow, bright as a beach bucket, the one the children propped on the handle of my garden shovel, just beyond the blooming bush. May fourth (or is it the fifth?) and the snow is at last gone from our valley—though there's plenty on the mountain, where die-hards are still skiing. And yesterday we finally broke through the last stubborn chunk of ice at our doorstep to unveil the shiny gray stones we've not seen for many months. The first daffodil has opened in the meadow and there are crocus now blooming where the snow blower was parked through the winter.

For the third day in a row our thermometer has crept over eighty in full sun, and our sleepy, frigid landscape has responded jubilantly. The forsythia has never bloomed like this before. Perhaps her spirit, like my own, is exhilarated by this sudden and total emancipation from winter's grip. I noticed the plethora of buds a couple days ago and brought Michael to the garden to see them. Standing there he shook his head and said, "Those are leaf buds; this bush never blooms." Wasn't he surprised last night when I walked him out to admire her stunning rebuttal?

All the early plants are starting to peek up from beneath their blanket of wood shavings and Bravo's manure. I love to walk slowly through the gardens this time of year, greeting each plant like an old friend I've not seen in such a while. Some of them are hard to recognize at first glance—their baby faces so unlike the mature countenances I said good-bye to last autumn when I cut the tall stalks and seed pods and bedded them down. Kind of like reminiscing through books of baby pictures: "That's what your smile looked like before you grew those big teeth." Everything now is tiny, delicate, giving no hint of the monstrous beauties they'll become.

Unfortunately, our bluebirds did not stay around to nest. I don't know if it is because of the construction. We weren't here to keep the swallows away from the bluebirds' boxes as we've done in other years—though I'm uncertain as to whether our shaking a towel or beating the air with a broomstick ever did much, other than entertain the neighbors. Anyway, there are swallows in all the boxes, bluebirds in none, and the construction on the last vacant lot has begun. The cement workers like honky-tonk western music and it blares out of their radios, drowning the springtime chorus I much prefer: wind chimes, rustling leaves, pond ripples lapping against the rock, frog song, and the sounds of many different birds.

Yesterday Ekta's violin melodies joined the rest of the wetlands music. It was her first day of practice since before our trip, and sweet to hear. She had had a bad spin with her violin in the weeks before we left. April 12 was Bravo's birthday (two weeks after Ekta's tenth, he turned three) and Ekta was concerned about him being away from home. We had just taken him to the training stable and she had cried and cried the night before, not wanting to be without him for a whole month. She was so worried that he would be unhappy there. She wanted to make his birthday special for him, so she planned to take him for a long romp away from his boarding school and then perform a violin concert for him.

She figured out how to play "Happy Birthday" and practiced it along with several other favorites. But in the days before the birthday concert a bad thing happened: her violin was defiled when the instructor allowed another child to use Ekta's violin for a lesson. This other girl routinely forgets to bring her instrument to school and, according to Ekta, never practices and doesn't even seem to care about the violin. So when her classmate found herself without a violin at lesson time and asked Ekta if she could use hers, Ekta said no and left the building for recess. When she returned, the girl was taking her lesson on Ekta's instrument.

Ekta was in a very foul mood when she got home from school that day and I suggested she play her violin, thinking how much she enjoys it. She resisted at first, then eventually got it out of the case and put it on her shoulder. But when she lifted it to her neck and tilted her chin against its shiny wood, she burst into tears. It didn't fit right. The girl had ruined it, she wailed, and through her tears the story came tumbling out. At bedtime she started crying about it again, and by the next morning she could think of little else.

So I called Ruth, her instructor. Fortunately, she understood right away. She said, "I feel the same way about my instrument, and I certainly would never let anybody else play it. I should have realized that about Ekta." Unfortunately, the girl did not tell Ruth that Ekta had said she couldn't use her instrument. But Ruth said it was her mistake not to talk with Ekta herself before letting anyone play her violin. "The minute Ekta walked into the room and saw the other student with her instrument, I knew I'd made a mistake," she added. "It's like someone asking me if they could sleep with my husband and I say no. Then I come home to discover them in bed together. That's how Ekta looked."

Ruth met with Ekta later that evening, and her apology helped alleviate Ekta's sense of betrayal, so I was hopeful. And grateful, too, for a wise teacher who understands the passions involved in making music.

Still, for almost two weeks Ekta cried every time she tried to practice, saying that her violin just didn't fit anymore and would never be right again. She did manage to perform Bravo's birthday concert, but after that she didn't play again. I'm hoping that our time away in Punta Cana will have helped her to recover from the insult and that once again her cheek will snuggle comfortably into position.

So that's our experience in music of late. It made me think about how important it is to let our feelings be what they are. So often, I try to talk myself into other feelings, reasoning with myself about why I shouldn't feel the way I do. I try to convince myself that if I were a better person I would realize such feelings are unnecessary. But in fact I usually end up feeling even worse, because then I'm not only upset about the situation, I also become upset about my reaction to it. So much better simply to allow my feelings to be what they are.

I went to visit Bravo on Tuesday. He's doing well with his training but did not seem happy. In fact, the trainer said he had been moping the week we were gone. If only we could have told him we'd be away just a week and would return, and that in twelve days he'd be with us again. I miss him terribly, too. He must feel upset and confused, not knowing why he's there or if he's ever coming home again. Communication is a great gift. Understanding, though it cannot alter the actual circumstances, can certainly free us up to experience things differently.

There's a strip along I-89 where mountains keep you company on both sides of the highway for quite a stretch. It's always interesting to watch the progress of the seasons in bands across their sloping hillsides. How things have changed since my last trip, when we were on our way to the airport. The mountains look younger now, their faces growing rosy with so many red buds forming on the silver-gray branches. Of course there are still the conifers with their age-old green of many seasons, but they do not command the attention that they did throughout the winter, when the other trees were bare.

As I was driving home I was feeling younger, too, and lighter—a bit more hopeful than I have for many months.

Barli had her baby, a little boy. He was born around one o'clock the night before we left, just after the candle I was burning for them refused to be extinguished. I blew it quite deliberately, several times; the flame flickered and rose up again. So I started praying really hard. I told myself: *Send all the love and courage you can muster, because right now she must be needing it.* So I did, and a short time later the candle extinguished with hardly a puff. The next morning she called to say her wee son was born around one in the morning. He's her fourth baby, her third boy. They only had names for a girl, so we didn't find out he was Simon Alexander until we got home from our trip.

Then we also found out that my mother caught a plane quickly when Barli came down with a terrible uterine infection. All of Barli's babies have been home births and she's never had a problem, but this one was a whopper. She ended up in the hospital in critical condition. My mother took the baby and camped out with two of Barli's friends, who offered to wet-nurse little Simon. When the lactation consultant said it finally would be OK for Barli to start nursing him herself, my mom and Simon moved into the hospital room with Barli, who had been miserable without her baby. Now everyone is home again and things are much better. My mother is planning to stay on for at least another week, and all should be well soon.

I think I mentioned to you that Barli is moving to New Hampshire in just a few weeks. Very difficult timing—all these major transitions on top of each other. She hasn't even seen the house they're buying, except on videotape. And the first offer on the house they're trying to sell fell through two days before Simon was born.

You're right, Christin, it does seem like only yesterday that she was a cute little bridesmaid at our wedding. And that was twenty years ago. Maybe we all should stop having birthdays, and just count every day as the immense blessing that it is.

10

Seedlings

Journal: Thursday in May, after Dartmouth

Beautifully warm and sunny. I came out to cut daffodils from the meadow, but there's a goose sitting there so I'll wait. It's funny: she's plopped right down in front of the flowers, her back to the water, as though she too were admiring them. I'll leave a couple out there for her.

I'm sitting on my chaise lounge and hoping to be able to sleep outside this afternoon. I've been on thyroid medicine for almost three weeks now and I am getting better. Though I still sleep every day, I am starting to have some energy again and I'm not feeling so impossibly tired and cold all the time. The diagnosis helped me break out of a very unhappy cycle of discouragement. What a blessing to discover that part of my fatigue is actually treatable and not just brain injury fatigue that I'll have to live with the rest of my life.

Our appointments at Dartmouth went well. Benjamin has improved slightly across all tests, so that is significant in itself. He is now ready for the next level of treatment, which I'll try to organize for six weeks this summer. I was sort of hoping that all would be at one hundred percent now and he'd be finished, but I guess that's unrealistic. Gradual improvement over a longer period of remediation is the likelier course. Dr. Musiek points out that once there is improvement in auditory processing, other aspects of cognitive processing will get better too. So things are moving in the right direction.

My own testing showed remarkable progress. Though I knew things were improving steadily, I was surprised at how much easier the listening and processing tasks were this time around and was especially pleased to see concrete evidence of the progress. I know that I'm doing better at home than I did six months ago, but sometimes I think that's just because of all the compensatory strategies that I have thoroughly integrated into my routines. To see that there are actual physical improvements in my brain is very hopeful.

Dr. Musiek was excited about the big gains. He explained to me that when there is neurological damage and subsequent retraining, the brain often will recruit a new bunch of neurons to take over for the old ones. They will be trained in the new line of work and then do it, while continuing former operations as well. Additionally, some of the damaged neurons may be healing and relearning their former tasks through this focused training regimen. What an awesome thing a brain is. Actually, our entire body is awesome.

Dr. Musiek is planning to publish a case study that he believes will be helpful in brain injury treatment, so he will do some further tests. While I'm happy to get the word out, I am a bit hesitant about becoming a case subject in the medical literature. I don't know why. I'll have to live with the question for a while.

I'm supposed to collect my notes regarding what has improved, in what ways, over the period of the treatment.

One thing I just noticed yesterday was that for the first time, while talking on the phone with my left ear to the receiver, I actually caught myself reflecting at the same time that I was processing what I heard. I had called someone to discuss a journal abstract I'd just read—that in itself a notable accomplishment—and as she was responding to my question I realized that I asked myself, *Is this new information? Is she telling me something I don't already know?* And then later: *Do I agree or disagree?*

As I assembled the notes and "to do" list in my conversation notebook after the phone call, I realized what a breakthrough that is. Not only was I listening well with my left ear (which used to jumble up the information it took in), I was listening and processing at the same time. It reminded me of the first time I caught myself having a tiny daydream while driving the van. Usually I had to be entirely immersed in the task of driving, with all mental energy focused on rehearsing over and over where I was going, talking directions out loud to myself, counting phone poles for depth perception and safe distances, reminding myself constantly to keep my eyes roving, etc. I never had any mental space available for conjuring up extraneous thoughts but one day, miraculously, it happened. I remember the exact strip of road. What a happy day that was!

Like yesterday, when I realized that not only was I on the phone—left-eared, processing accurately—but I was thinking and analyzing at the same time. WOW!

Journal: Saturday, May 19, 2001

My birthday! I'm forty-two today.

The lilacs are covered with buds, but it's still too cold for them to open. It's a gray, rainy day, and I'm snuggled cozily into my new afghan from Minnow. It's made of silver-green yarn, the color of moss on my garden rocks, but soft as a newborn baby's fuzzy head. I'm lying here wondering if everyone likes her own birthday month as much as I like May: lilacs, apple blossoms, rhubarb pie, high school proms, and dandelion-covered lawns.

Last Sunday we had a quite perfect Mothers Day. After breakfast in bed (with everyone joining me), Michael and Benjin worked on the garden railroad while Ekta and I worked at the barn. Bravo came home the day before; it's so great to have him with the family again. He's doing really well, too, behaving a little more like a horse and less like a king—not so bossy in the barnyard. He thinned down slightly, and since he's healthier at this weight, we're going to try to maintain his new diet. Unfortunately, he takes his eating very seriously and will likely be disappointed not to have a full-time schedule of keeping the meadow mowed down—a meadow that was intended to pasture two full-sized horses.

Later in the morning we headed to the nursery. It was great timing, as we were the only ones there. I like to be alone with the plants while I quietly determine who might like to come home to my garden. In the afternoon, Benjin finished setting up his track and we had the inaugural running of the railroad—immensely exciting after all these months of planning! He was concerned that the grade in one part might be too steep, but Mighty Mac, his cute yellow engine, chugged along capably.

Then we sprayed the wildflower meadows. I've never done it before, and I'm wondering what organic gardeners would say about the maneuver. As with all things, it's a tricky balance. We put the meadows in with full commitment to environmental stewardship—so much better than mowing an acre of lawn, and clearly the best way to provide natural habitat. But over the past four or five years, goldenrod, sedge, and other aggressive grasses have begun to overtake the meadows. The horticulturalist at the wildflower farm where I bought the seeds says we have two choices: completely start over (and lose all the established plants) or use a mild herbicide to kill the grasses. They spray their meadows when necessary and then do a fair amount of replanting to group the wildflowers into colonies that can better resist the invading grasses. We'll try that and see what happens this year before going to more drastic measures. In either case, the goldenrod is here to stay; it releases a toxin from its roots that prevents other plants from moving in. And the herbicide won't kill it. I wonder why goldenrod comes so well-equipped, what purpose it serves in the evolution of things.

Minnow and Bobba came for dinner. Minnow had just returned from Chicago, where Barli is on the mend and little Simon Alexander is thriving. Minnow looked quite exhausted and uncomfortable; we've since found out that she has a strep infection. I wonder if it's something she got from Barli. I gave her an overnight stay at a bed-and-breakfast as a Mothers Day gift. She has devoted so much of herself to caring for her family lately; I wanted her to have a well-deserved, self-indulgent getaway. I don't know if she'll want to do it, but I thought it was worth suggesting. I don't think we mothers are very good at self-indulgence, though, and it's likely that even if she did manage to arrive at the inn she wouldn't feel right about enjoying herself there all alone. Feeling needed has its own set of rewards, and we're unlikely to relinquish them easily.

Michael completely outdid himself for dinner—surf and turf, with lobsters for the mothers and steak for the others. My gift was a shiny evergreen-colored wheelbarrow, and nothing could have pleased me more. Funny to be so delighted with a wheelbarrow; kind of like Michael's excitement over a new snow shovel. A wheelbarrow does suggest labor-intensive pursuits, yet is so much better than a vacuum cleaner! After dinner, Bobba hung the screened door he'd made for the chicken coop—another marvelous gift, as I will now be spared many encounters with chicken droppings in all the wrong places.

Bobba and Minnow ended up staying overnight so she could go to the clinic the next day. And since Bobba was here on a Monday morning, we loaded up a month's worth of recycling. It had begun to create an obstacle course along the path to the washing machine, and he generously offered to cart it all off in his red truck, the one with that nasty "Take Back Vermont" bumper sticker. Michael covers it with duct tape whenever he drives that truck around. Odd, isn't it, that the dad I love so much could post that detestable slogan?

The saying came into vogue during our last election, I think mostly as a way of protesting the recently-enacted civil union legislation for homosexual couples. There were also some hotly contested proposals for education funding reforms and land conservation. So there was a big "Take Back Vermont" thrust last November. Thankfully, those candidates were defeated. But the bumper stickers are still around, and there are days when I've got one parked in my own yard.

What good can possibly come of such intolerance? I don't know—any more than I can figure out why there has to be a plethora of goldenrod in my meadow. Why is it that the friendlier daisies, graceful lupine, or healing echinacea can't hold more ground?

So here it is, the morning of my forty-second birthday (lunchtime, actually) and I'm still in pajamas, thoroughly enjoying the pace of a drizzly gray morning to hang out in bed and write. Michael is at the clinic, Benjin is reading for his Viking report, and Ekta is illustrating her main lesson book. In a few moments I'll get dressed in my new birthday shirt—a sky blue long-sleeved cotton tee, covered with vines and roses all over the top. For lunch, I'll eat rhubarb pie and nothing else, so it'll be a big serving.

Then I'll see what the rest of the day holds.

E-MAIL: TO CHRISTIN
DATE: MAY 30, 2001

As you know, sweet Christin, I received a most wonderful birthday letter from you. And then I had a call from Paul, my New York artist friend. I don't remember if you know him. We met at Holy Names in California. We were next door neighbors in the dormitory and had the easy intimacy that a married woman can enjoy with a gay man. I love him dearly. We're both May babies, so we share birthday greetings. We also sing to each other at Thanksgiving. One will call the other with "Over the River and Through the Woods" the whole song, both verses. Rituals like that are great comforts. I especially remember the Thanksgiving right after my accident. Paul sang to my answering machine and I played it over and over again in the days that followed. I wonder if most people understand how vital those simple gestures are.

On my birthday, he said he had always been impressed by my artistry, that my "creative energy is astounding" to him. I have those words scribbled right here in my conversation book, where I was writing quickly to keep up. Then he said, "I've wondered what place that creative spirit will find in your new life. Like a seedling that needs to push itself up some day: where will it come up, and how will it look?"

That question intrigued me. It's something I've been grappling with, of course, but never quite articulated to myself as clearly as he did that day. As you know, much of my life now is completely structured. For a long time, I resisted all that "boxing in"—every hour mapped out, every random thought and piece of information recorded and filed appropriately. I've grown used to it now; in fact I'm actually comforted by the charts and lists that order my life these days. When Paul posed that question about my creativity, an answer surfaced within me almost immediately.

The seedling is pushing its way up between the pages of my notebooks, in the writing that I began as cognitive retraining for my injured brain and that has since become a kaleidoscope through which I view the whole experience. I collect tiny moments of my life, like seashells from the beach, and I play with them in my mind. Over and over, I practice remembering, seeing how some things connect to other things. I look for words to put my pictures into sentences, and then the little pieces of life slowly take shape on a page. My brain works slowly but at least it's working, and I realize now that if it were working quickly, I probably wouldn't be writing; I would be doing all the other things I used to do. That would be very nice, but right now this feels like a precious opportunity. I must enjoy this time where healing through writing is my creative work.

So when Paul asked that question I told him I was writing. He said, "Isn't that amazing? I think somehow I knew you would be writing."

I felt good about that. Legitimate.

My birthday ended stupendously. When I went with Michael and the children to do barn chores, they slid back the door on the tractor shed to reveal a new bicycle. For me!

The black seat has the letters COMFORT inscribed in silver and there are enough gears to propel me over any terrain from here to the moon and back. I was a little uncertain at first, a little wobbly, but the kids rode along beside me, offering technical assistance with the gears and much encouragement. Then they headed back home to help Michael finish chores and I set off down the road. I went all the way out to the paved highway before turning back, pedaling toward the setting sun.

I can't tell you how many years it's been since I was a kid with a new bike on my birthday. Remember the excitement, and that moment of sheer bliss when you discover you can actually ride it? Heading home, I focused on the shining mountains and laughed out loud to no one but the wind.

So my dear Christin, that brings you to date—through May 19 anyway. I'm still sorting out the days since then. It's time for me to go lie down so I'll be ready for the children this afternoon.

Please be well out there where you are.

Humility

11

Regeneration

Journal: June 23, Saturday at the ocean

York Beach, Maine on a thickly foggy day. It's about noon and I'm waiting to meet up with Barli. They're driving up from New Hampshire to meet us and take my niece Bethany home after her little vacation here with us. The girls are down at the water and I can barely see them through the mist. Ekta's in the waves with her boogie board and Bethany is collecting starfish. She has found two with only four legs each. Starfish are amazing at regeneration; imagine losing a leg and becoming two complete beings instead of one!

I have just finished Lucy Grealy's *Autobiography of a Face.* I am glad Christin recommended it. Aside from the healing aspects I gained from her exquisite narrative, the process of simply completing a book cover to cover is so uplifting. It's the first time I've been able to follow a story and hold onto it long enough for the words to find an anchor in my brain. I can do quite well with these personal chronicles, moving forward from a single point of view—and what a unique, terribly painful point of view she has! What a struggle to overcome her feelings about her freakishness. Imagine needing thirty operations to repair a jawline, creating new bone and skin that was eventually reabsorbed by her body anyway. As I sit here with Bethany's starfish beside me in a Frisbee filled with sand and water, I'm thinking about Grealy's endless hospital stays. I marvel at how the only thing needed for the starfish's regenerative process is enough sand and water to make a sea-bottom home.

Yesterday the girls and Michael caught a flounder that was stranded in a small pool of water on the beach when the tide went out. It's an odd-looking creature, with two eyes on one side of its body and everything else out of position in relation to the eyes. Many centuries ago the flounder swam like any other fish in the sea—upright, with eyes and fins on each side of its body and a tail and mouth that worked in a motion perpendicular to the ocean floor. But over the course of eons it gradually came to swim only on its side, mouth and tail running parallel to the sandy bottom in which it hid itself. Eventually, the eye on its underside grew into a new position next to its other eye on the top of its body.

I wonder: given the opportunity to reflect, would the flounder feel freakishly ugly or uniquely beautiful? And what would these four-legged starfish think?

E-MAIL: TO CHRISTIN
DATE: JUNE 27, 2001

Christin dearest,

It is not you who have been neglectful; I'm the one who is so tardy in responding. You did in fact send a delightful birthday gift—pages from your rewrite. I can't imagine figuring out a new way to tell the story and then just starting over.

You are amazing, and I always love your writing. That image from your last e-mail is breathtaking: "the silken sunshine ribbon unraveling in her lap."

Your agent's recommendation that you tell the story in chronological order is interesting in that it would actually affect the artistry of the novel and your vision. It is also interesting because I have discovered that the only kind of fiction I can read is chronological. If a narrative starts at a moment in time and moves forward in orderly sequence from only one point of view, I can grasp it. Otherwise no. I think that's why I have not been able to digest *Altar Music,* a much more complex novel. I am doing pretty well now with journals and memoirs.

I am a little curious, because in my professional work I used to synthesize life stories quite well from very different starting places and several points of view. The therapist usually starts with here and now and then goes backward and around many paths to piece together a life story and an understanding of the client. I do see how you could discover a story that way and then start all over, figuring out a structure to tell it; the true writing of it begins even later. I hope you are enjoying the work. I know you are nicely caught up in it.

Recently I have been nicely caught up in my children's lives for the most part. The ending of school was a terrific whirlwind and then we were in Maine for a couple days at the ocean. Now we are home again and they go to soccer camp every day, which means a lot of driving for me. My doctor has increased my thyroid medication twice, and it looks like the hormone levels are about right. My hair is still falling out in huge gobs, and I'm thinking I might have to cut it. But other symptoms are slowly dissipating, and I'm doing really well. I am at once celebrating my ability to keep up with my children's busy schedules and longing for some leisurely lie-around-in-the-hammock time.

Today Michael is in the hammock, studying for the re-certification exams that he takes in Boston on July 14. We don't have any gloriously old and shady trees like yours; our hammock hangs in an alcove of our deck, in sunlight softly filtered by the pergola with morning glories. One good thing about having it right here at the house is that it gets well used. And that was my goal when we purchased it on a trip to L.L.Bean in Maine several summers ago. The sales clerk told us about a man who had been in the store earlier that week, standing next to the hammock, dreamily admiring it. The clerk asked if he would like to try it out and the man told him, "No, I already have one. I bought it here a couple of years ago. I've never been in it, and I was thinking maybe I should slow down."

When the salesman told me that story, I decided the best part of this Fathers Day gift would not be the hammock itself but a promise to make sure that Michael spends many fine hours in it. These past couple of years the kids and I have taken that duty to heart, and his hammock has been well-used—up until today, when he climbed into it and started reviewing pediatric cardiology. Although I guess even that's OK. It is a glorious summer day, and so much better to be studying at home in the hammock than in some generic conference room at a review seminar in Atlanta or Seattle.

I've just returned from errands in town and was happily surprised to see your e-mail, to know that your bluebirds are safe and that Rita the dog is guarding them in earnest. I want to write all the snippets of conversations I've had with you in my mind over the last few weeks, yet I know that will have to wait until things settle down a bit here. At least I did want to respond right away to say you have not been neglectful and also to say thank you for writing whenever you can. Your letters always make me feel you are close by, and your words give me something lovely to work with, sparkling images that I carry around in my head, teasing those neurons into firing away. I know the healing is happening.

Do you remember how Joseph Chilton Pierce wrote that we must tell stories to children, because the stories actually develop their brains by creating neural pathways and connections? I first read his stuff right before I went to work at the orphanage in Bangladesh, over twenty years ago. Neurological research since then has well supported his theory.

Journal: Saturday morning after soccer camp

Nine a.m. and I'm delighted to have nothing on the calendar after being totally wiped out from the week—two-hour round trips to Craftsbury twice a day, plus summer hockey on top of that. It's been my utter undoing. I wondered if maybe something had gone awry with my thyroid medication, but Michael said it's more likely that I'm underestimating the extent of my brain injury fatigue.

Perhaps. I've been doing well for so many weeks, I sort of forgot how intense it can be. I need to realize that whenever I'm in my usual routine I can do amazingly well, but when that routine changes, my brain is overtaxed. It was a little disappointing—actually a lot disappointing—to be confronted with such debilitating fatigue again after thinking that perhaps I was done with that robber forever. But it's also reassuring to know that as long as I stay within my own familiar boundaries and well-rehearsed patterns, I can do fine. I just need to lower my expectations.

This is the weekend when, ten years ago, I flew home from Bangkok with two wee babies in my arms: Ekta and Kamla, the little girl I was escorting to her parents in Minneapolis. I know this time well, even without a calendar. So does Ekta, because the yellow primrose starts blooming. That's the flower Benjamin planted for her the day after she arrived home. The lady at the Brick House Bookstore had lots of primrose flowering in her garden and gave him some after he told her about his new sister. We've always called it "Ekta's coming home flower." In fact, I didn't know its real name until recently.

The birds in the nest below my bedroom window are noisy, noisy this morning. Barely hatched, they don't even resemble birds yet, just mouths—four bright reddish-pink and very wide mouths, shrilly shrieking as their mother comes and goes. Relatively speaking, they'll be tiny for such a short time; I wonder if their red-capped sparrow mother savors this precious time or is merely exhausted.

The other morning, Benjamin hugged me as I packed his lunch for soccer camp and said, "You're getting smaller and smaller. You used to be much bigger."

"No, honey," I replied. "It's you who used to be much smaller."

I remember when we moved here he wasn't much above my knees. When the fireflies made their seasonal debut he'd disappear in the tall grass, chasing after them. He wanted to catch some for Ekta, who was coming from India very soon. He placed a jarful in the window beside her crib "to light her way."

Now here they are, ten and twelve years old, running around the soccer field. All I do is the driving and the sandwich making, and I'm getting "smaller and smaller."

Ekta was terribly unhappy as we left camp yesterday because her team, "Southern Brazil," placed last in their "World Cup" games.

"And Northern Brazil kept bragging, Mom. It's no fair. They had all the good players," she lamented—over and over until finally I told her to stop. I reminded her that winning is not the most important thing. It's important to be a good sport, I said, at which point she burst into tears. I brought her to the car, where we could talk privately.

"Ekta, there are some things in life that matter a whole lot and other things that don't matter so much. That soccer game you just played is one of those things that don't matter so much."

"Well, it matters to me!" she protested loudly. I was surprised; she had never before been so attached to the outcome of a game.

"Does it feel really important to you?" I asked. She nodded her head. I hugged her close and said, "Ekta, I love you so much. Whether you play soccer or don't play soccer, whether you win or lose, whether you're a good sport or not, I always love you and I'm sorry this game feels so disappointing to you."

As her sobbing subsided I asked, "Why did you want to win? Does it feel really important to be the best?"

"I don't need to be the best," she replied. "I just don't want to be in last place. Northern Brazil was really bragging and it hurt my feelings. I'm not good at soccer and I was always last in the running races, too. Every morning, I was in last place. I don't want to be last all the time."

What could I do or say to make this any easier? When the cruel realities of the world press in on my children, threatening to suffocate their tender souls, I feel hopelessly ill-prepared for this job called motherhood. I just sat there with my daughter, her head against my shoulder, her black curls blowing across my cheek, and stared at the sweet william blossoming along the path to the playing fields. I noticed it was the same variety of sweet william as in our garden at home, fuchsia and white, almost polka-dotted. Ekta had pointed it out to me the night before, saying that it looked like a "whole bouquet all by itself." She was sitting on my overturned weeding bucket, playing her violin while I transplanted our sunflower seedlings.

The rest of the soccer players cleared the fields. As I watched the last of them go, I tried to guess whether any more discussion would be helpful to Ekta. "I wonder if maybe you're feeling a little like Benjamin felt at the chess tournament." She nodded yes and snuggled in closer.

Benjamin was devastated by his experience. The tournament was in February and he didn't play chess again until this summer's trip to Maine. In retrospect, I should never have let them go to the state championships as their first-ever competitive event, but that was the tournament their chess leader had arranged for the club. Ekta actually placed third in her age group, though I don't think she would have cared at that time had she not placed at all.

But Benjamin was pretty much blown away by the level of competition among the older kids, many of whom were nationally ranked. In the days leading up to the tournament he had been asking what would happen if he beat all the other players. I answered his questions, all the while suggesting that usually the people who win those tournaments have been playing chess a lot longer than he. All the same, I think he had dreams of being a champion. What a fiasco the tournament was for him. And unfortunately it came at a time when he was becoming acutely aware of his learning challenges in a way that he never had been before.

So I'm sitting here thinking this is the same story for Ekta. Right now we are heavily engrossed in trying to help her make some progress with reading and writing. She is starting in a new school in September. She's worried about being a fifth-grader who can't read, and yesterday's soccer experience certainly didn't do much for her self-esteem. This morning my heart aches for the kids who don't fall into the "above average" category on any of the measurable criteria that seem so important in our society.

One of the great gifts of this head injury—having been stripped of many capabilities—is the liberating experience of feeling loved for who I am instead of for what I do. Perhaps even better than that is the humility that comes from realizing I'm not capable of excelling at just any endeavor I might now choose. I'm starting to know, in a way I simply couldn't have known before, what it might feel like to stand in my children's shoes as the world mirrors back their rankings in the classroom, at the chess table, or on the soccer field. I'm certainly committed to holding up a different mirror whenever they'll let me. I want them to see themselves truly: the unique beauty of their souls, not the contorted image that society's warped lenses produce. It's a struggle though, isn't it, not to be defined by how we perform, what we accomplish, who others tell us we are?

I'm tired now and must rest again, so will store this and return to this topic a little later, hopefully before the holiday fireworks begin.

Journal: July 6, 2001

Well it's now July 6 and the red-white-and-blue is all done. We went down to my parents' for their town celebration and Barli came too. So we had a big crowd—her six, our four, and my parents. And our VW, Ladybug, of course, driving Miss Lillian.

After last year's parade she fell and broke her hip, then developed pneumonia in the hospital and eventually came home to die. But try as she might, she couldn't die. Finally, she figured out that God had other plans for her, so she set her mind and body to a truly arduous, lengthy rehabilitation. She's ninety-four years old, and throughout the long recuperation her will to live fluctuated pretty regularly. That was quite exasperating to those who were close to her. They grew impatient with her decisions, which seemed to change with the wind. But in the end she made it home to the village green and there she was: back in Ladybug, leading the Fourth of July parade.

When the prizes were awarded for the floats, Miss Lillian received "Best Comeback of the Year." She looked terrifically grand, and I expect she is happy to be here.

After the parade and the band concert on the green, the kids did sack races and egg-on-a-spoon walks. Barli and I showed Ekta and Bethany how to hop in the middle of the stride for the three-legged race. The girls practiced until they got it, and then they won the race. They returned to us wearing blue ribbons and big smiles. And the nice thing about those races is that all the other kids got ribbons too, red ones.

Benjamin and Michael helped cart many boxes of books back into the library after the book sale on the green. I think they put out the same cartons of dusty old things every year and maybe make six or eight dollars, but it's the tradition. Then we helped the ladies at the chicken barbecue finish off the Ben & Jerry's ice cream so it wouldn't melt.

After that, we went to Minnow and Bobba's for swimming and another cookout. But we were rained out. Bobba ended up cooking the cheeseburgers from the bedroom window, because if he stood outside he'd have been blown away. We drove home in pelting rain that subsided just as we arrived in Stowe. The children were able to watch spectacular fireworks from their beds—the kind that look like cosmic exploding dandelions.

I was thinking it's such a gift simply to be here, to be alive, and an even greater blessing to be aware of the gift and to treasure it every day. Michael was in the emergency room yesterday with a patient who was having a heart attack. While he sat there, an ambulance came in with a suicide victim. A thirty year-old man had shot himself in the head but still had a heartbeat. Today the transplant team is harvesting his organs.

Compassion

12

Terrible Days

E-mail: To Christin
Date: Some day after September 11, 2001

Sweet Christin, dearest friend,

Such a warm embrace you sent me yesterday. I too have been speechless, not able to offer anything into the mournful silence. And I haven't tried to, really, because it has seemed quite impossible to craft any words. I am so grateful for your letter, since I have been often with you in spirit. Now to hold you on paper is a deep comfort.

As you could imagine, I'm not quick enough with the reasoning skills one needs to process these events, though I don't imagine any human brain has the neural framework sufficient to grasp such unimaginable atrocities. Nor do I feel equipped to contemplate the various opinions regarding our response. Besides which, so much of this evil seems to have sprung from my own beloved, mysterious, and magnificent birth land, from an Islamic people whom I knew to be fiercely faithful and hospitable, just and charitable friends. How has such hatred grown?

I fear for my children, whose ethnic appearance could make them vulnerable to rash actions. I never leave them now, except in school or with friends. Michael said last week, "Remember when the hardest thing we had to talk about was helping them make the transition to a new school, figure out what soccer team to play on, and how to squeeze in Ekta's orchestra rehearsals? Doesn't that seem like a long-ago world?"

Given the three-hour difference between eastern and pacific time, I'm imagining that you woke to a country already in shock. I woke that morning like every other morning, except that day I had an appointment to get my hair cut, an effort to remedy my thyroid fall-out. September 11 was at that moment significant only in that I had not cut my hair since I was in my early teens.

As you know, we don't own a TV or subscribe to a newspaper, and we almost never turn on the radio. I took the children to school, came home to barn chores and laundry, paid some bills, and cleaned the kitchen. Then I headed out for my appointment. I walked into the hair shop and there was a little TV on the counter, tuned to CNN. "Hey, what's up?" I asked. "Is there something going on?"

"Oh my God, PJ, you don't know!" Lisa said. "You haven't heard: America is being attacked! The Trade Towers in New York have just fallen. Hijacked commercial jets flew into them and exploded. Another one hit the Pentagon. One plane is still lost, hijacked. Sit down here." I sat in the chair and stared at our reflections in the mirror. I was speechless.

She wrapped a dark plastic sheet around my neck and continued relaying what she had learned from the TV. Slowly, things began to sink in. "Is this an emergency?" I asked her. "Is there something we should be doing right now?" It seemed inconceivable to me that something so huge could be happening and I was sitting in a beautician's chair.

She tried to sound reassuring. "I don't think so. Now, what about your hair?"

My hair, I thought. *Oh yes, I'm here to have it cut.* But I couldn't think about that now. I had to go to the school and make sure my children were safe. I had to call Michael and ask him what to do. Find out if my friend Paul is safe. Pray for him—isn't his new apartment right by the Trade Towers?

"Cut the bottom off my ponytail. Just make it straight," I told her without thinking much about it. She explained that if she simply cut the bottom of the ponytail straight off, my hair would actually be uneven. I decided it really didn't matter; I wanted the quickest haircut I could get and to be on my way.

I drove by the school, where everything appeared normal. When I returned home, I called Michael. Then I turned on the radio until I could stand it no longer, and headed out to the barn where Bravo, in his slightly furry autumn coat, stood with his usual impatience while I brushed him. How could everything seem so normal, when all this was going on? It makes me think of a massive creature—a dragon—mortally injured, whose parts keep moving a while before the stillness of death sets in. That's how it was here, until gradually we grasped the truth of the terror.

How lucky I am to have my children, my precious children, at a time like this. They help me to believe in a better future. How can one possibly mother her children without that hope in her heart? And so I must be faithful to that promise no matter what evil, what darkness, may be rising around us. I do my best to answer their questions, which are also my questions, only more simply stated and more insightful out of their innocence.

I am sorry for you, dear Christin, that you have been ill with this. Yes, our bodies most certainly do express our souls. If I did not have my Benjamin and Ekta to care for, I can't imagine what shape I'd be in. Maintaining a familiar routine that keeps them grounded has been an important part of making them feel secure. Trying to orchestrate that has kept me grounded as well.

At first, Ekta couldn't get straight what had happened. What she heard from her classmates didn't make sense. Having been to NYC, having flown on planes, she couldn't put together how those buildings could fall down and how the pilots could make such a big mistake. Eventually she moved her thinking out of the genre of catastrophic accidents and into the realm of good guys and bad guys, where the bad guys actually wanted to crash the buildings. But that still didn't hold together, because in all her imaginings, there are no bad guys who would want to do that. She said she wished we had a TV so she could see what the kids in her class saw, and then she would understand it.

Michael brought home a newspaper and showed her photos of the crashes and the explosions; she drew her own pictures and diagrams with planes and pilots. At dinner, she said she was hoping there wouldn't be any children whose mommies and daddies didn't come home that night. And if there were children without parents, what would happen to them? She asked if I would be going to New York to help them. I assured her we would do our best to help, but that I would stay here in Vermont. She also was worried about animals that wouldn't have their owners anymore. We have since found out that shelters here are helping with overflow for the NYC animals that have been displaced. Often since the tragedy, Ekta will spontaneously light a candle and say, "Mom, let's have a minute of silence for all those people."

Unlike Ekta, who is immediately in touch with the raw pain of it all and actually able to carry it deep in her being, Benjamin can't take in too much of the suffering. He can't bear the human consequences of such violence and hatred, and does not want to hear about it or talk about it. Yet he was desperate for information at first. Every day when I picked him up after school he wanted to know what the news was. I started listening to news reports so I could fill him in. But as much as he seemed to need the information, he became angry when I offered the latest troubling developments. Of course none of the news was good, and in retrospect I think that is what he desperately was seeking.

I figured that out one day when I told him that the newscaster had interviewed the director of a relief organization, who reported they had a mini-disaster on their hands because of all the donations they had received. There wasn't enough storage space to accommodate all the hard hats, socks, work boots, food, and water bottles that were arriving by the truckload. Benjamin's face brightened. "You see, that just shows how much people care. Isn't that a really great kind of problem to have? That will show the terrorists something."

He continues to read the newspapers (we now buy them once a week) and is mostly consumed with figuring out who did it, if there are any new clues, and whether the world is safe yet. At night he stares off into space—from the bathroom skylight, on the way back from the barn, or sometimes lying on the warm hood of the car. A few nights after the tragedy he told us, "Some day the Big Dipper will change, and some day there won't even be a North Star." That's a striking thought. Perhaps it offers some small comfort to a twelve year-old boy, a boy who feels like the whole world is different now, prey to an evil force that turns planes full of people into missiles of mass destruction.

From a cosmological perspective, I wonder how the attacks looked. If stars come and go, exploding into new creations, perhaps we on this tiny Earth will become something cosmically beautiful through such dire events, whether man-made and terrible or natural and cataclysmic. Or are we—as you speculate, dear Christin—truly in the grip of original sin? And will the North Star simply be plucked from our sky by hands of retribution? I am just so happy to have your letter to respond to, someone to whom I can pour out my heart.

I am remembering a conversation I had with my Ekta many months ago. This happened sometime back in February, a time that I refer to as the "old world" because September 11 had not yet happened and my greatest distress lay within my own psyche.

I was in rough shape, feeling I would not be much good for anything ever again. I had just moved out of my counseling office and my yet-undiagnosed thyroid problems were in full operation. I was quite depressed and couldn't seem to find a way to turn things around for the better, but was trying my best not to be teary in front of the children. Then one night at dinner Benjamin asked if I was ever going to work again. We had been talking about Helen, who can't possibly stay in bed past five in the morning because she has so much work to do. Benjamin wanted to know when I would be "normal again" like Helen is, like I used to be. I left the table because I just couldn't handle that question without bursting into tears. Michael navigated the conversation while I worked on the dishes.

Later that night Ekta said, "I think there must be some feelings that have no words."

"Maybe so, Ekta. What do you mean?"

"When I was little and I had a feeling that didn't match up to any words, I just thought that I hadn't learned all the words yet. And I thought that when I got older, I would know the words for all the feelings, because I would learn them. But I'm old now and I know all the words, and it still seems like there are some feelings that just don't have any words. Is that right?"

"Yes, Ekta." I drew her into my lap as I sat down in my rocker. "You are absolutely right, and so wise too. Sometimes things happen and we feel so much, there are just no words." I held her close while we rocked, and I sang to her.

After a time, she said sleepily, "Mom, if someone didn't know you, like didn't know that you really are a person, they would think you're an angel. Because when you sing you sound like an angel."

In these bleak September days—when most assuredly there are no words for such feelings of unbearable loss—perhaps, in the midst of our turmoil, we must sing like angels. Dearest Christin, please take precious care of your shattered imagination; the world needs it. Curl up in your fuzzy blue robe that makes me think of morning glories, look again at the beauty around you, and write when you can.

In the meantime, keep praying for us all. You are especially good at that. And remember I love you, so greatly.

E-MAIL: TO CHRISTIN
DATE: NOVEMBER 6, 2001

Sweet birthday wishes to you, beloved Christin, at sixty-one,

Such a chilly day we are having, and so dark. The clouds look like the fur on our tiny ash gray kittens. It's so windy out there this morning that everything's billowing around like kittens too, first one direction and then the opposite.

We haven't "talked" in a long time. I'm hoping that you are well, and that your broken heart is piecing itself back together in the wake of September 11. Time has a way of distancing the pain and I am grateful for that, yet I don't think I would have us fall so far into our familiar lives that we forget the suffering. There is so much, worldwide.

We used to be taught that humans are genetically coded for altruism; it's a survival instinct, assuring the continuation of our species. I remember how empowering that felt when I first learned it in Social Psychology so many years ago. These days, I find myself often returning to that notion for reassurance. And I wonder: if we ignore the pain too much, are we at risk of diminishing that altruistic response? There is a saying from India, from the villages: "You can wake a truly sleeping person, but you cannot wake a person who pretends to be sleeping."

The sky is doing funny things now. Brilliant sun rays are breaking through the thick clouds and, because everything else is so dark, the light is almost blinding as it hits my computer screen and covers this letter with shadow lace from my curtain. That's good, because I'm getting too ponderous for a birthday greeting; it's nice to be interrupted.

Our kittens arrived Halloween night. The children woke to a total surprise the morning of All Souls' Day. They came with a note that said, "Found these in the forest and they're too young to ride with me past the moon. Please take good care of them." Ekta is convinced they arrived on the broomstick of a witch. But Benjamin recognized the grapefruit juice carton they were nestled into and later asked me where I got them. Our neighbor up the road had taken in a pregnant stray. She wanted these twins to stay together, and I decided we could probably have barn cats despite my allergy. Benjamin said, "Let's not tell Ekta. Let's not ruin her magic."

And magic it is for all of us. They are too tiny to be barn cats now, so they're living room cats (and Brandy is a guest room dog) for the time being. The kittens' names are Shadow and Moon and they have entirely opposite personalities—a lot like Benjamin and Ekta. On field trips to the barn, Moon is bold and dangerously gregarious while Shadow snuggles into Benjamin's fleece with only her head peeking out. We have our work cut out for us to get everyone on congenial terms by next spring, when hopefully they will move in with the rest of the fuzzy and feathered crew.

This afternoon Benjamin will ride the school bus for the first time, and he'll walk home to make his own dinner and pack up for ice hockey in Stowe. A friend will pick him up and drive him to practice because I'll be twenty miles away, taking Ekta to orchestra rehearsal. I'm a little nervous—funny how tiny moments in life mark big transitions. We raise our children not to need us. Then, when it happens, we feel displaced. Although I don't feel too displaced yet.

This morning, when I dropped Benjamin off, he asked yet again which bus to get on. I took a pen and wrote it on his hand, which is bigger than mine now. I wrote "Bus #1" along a crease in his palm—the one you can look at to count how many children a person will have when they grow up. Then under that line, I wrote Michael's phone number at the clinic. He is at the hospital now, delivering a baby, but the woman is pushing. So by the time Benjin might need to call, the baby should have arrived and Michael will be back at the clinic.

Well, that's life in our household today, Christin dearest. And I hope that life in your household is just perfect for many birthday blessings. Lovely, sweet surprises—the kind that come on chilly November mornings and warm your heart, like two kittens purring in a tiny scrap of sunshine on the couch.

Hope

13

Bravery and Dreams

E-MAIL: TO CHRISTIN
DATE: FEBRUARY 6, 2002

Good morning dear Christin,

Seems like forever since we've had a decent conversation. As you know, things got really busy here after my dad fell and shattered his hip. But now I'm happy to report that he's finally been able to return home. Thank you for all your kind thoughts and prayers, and for continuing to write even when I couldn't.

I'm sitting at my desk with a cup of tea. Tea of Good Tidings, it's called, a Christmas gift from my sister. This is a momentous occasion for me: I just made an appointment with a Vocational Rehabilitation counselor; I think I'm ready to start exploring my options. We meet next Monday, and I'll see what happens.

Yesterday I made chicken soup for Gretchen. She's in the midst of a new round of chemo for the brain tumor. Because of the nausea, she eats tiny amounts frequently, so I made itty-bitty muffins, the kind I used to make for my wee babes.

It's always a blessing when Gretchen lets me offer a small kindness. She doesn't realize it. She says things like, "I don't want to trouble you and I don't want you to fuss over me. I'm doing fine, really." Then I have to say, "Please, Gretchen. Please let me do something nice for you; I want to. And I promise I won't go to any trouble. How about some soup?"

She says, "I only like things plain, very plain," so I ask about potato soup, and she hesitates just long enough for me to figure out that she's going to say yes—even though she'd rather eat mud—just because that's the kind of sweet, gentle person she is. So quickly I suggest chicken soup and she tells me not to go to any trouble, so then I know she would like chicken soup.

I had to go to the grocery store twice, because I went without a shopping list the first time. I bought a mini rose plant that I saw when I walked in the door; Gretchen loves gardens. Then I bumped into a huge display of overly ripe avocados with envelope-size packets of guacamole mix tucked in all around them, so I bought some of those, too, because it seemed a shame to let so many ripe avocados go to waste. Then I remembered the chicken soup and picked up a bag of celery. At the checkout I bought some beautifully wrapped chocolate bars, then headed home.

Settled into my kitchen, I started chopping the celery and moved into a different realm of mindfulness. That's Gretchen's gift when she allows me to do this simple thing for her. From the window above my sink I can look over at her house. I'm startled to remember that two years ago I almost felt envious of her. After her brain tumor was removed she returned to her work pretty quickly and I wished I could too.

On my second journey for soup ingredients—with a proper list—I decided to go to a different grocer and I passed the book store, where my order was in. So I came home with

How to Write a Book Proposal, along with chicken, carrots, noodles, and broth. I actually ordered that book after visiting the drug store last week. Thinking I might try writing for a magazine, I purchased an armful to peruse. But I soon realized that most of their topics don't appeal to me. So I guess I'll just have to write a book.

I'm starting to understand what you were talking about, my wise and wonderful Christin, when you told me simply to write: write what I love and don't worry about the outcome. As soon as I start thinking about magazine articles, books, and publishers, I get very far away from the joy of writing. Worrying about whether someone will want to read what I write distracts me from what my soul is yearning to express. And the other thing I notice is that I start feeling this sense of urgency—like I have to figure this out right now and do it very soon, before somebody else does and I miss my opportunity. How crazy is that? I remember you saying, "You don't have to hurry with anything. You have the whole rest of your life."

I think all this may be coming up for me because of vocational rehab. Things are starting to move around in my psyche, and I'm becoming a little anxious and sad about work again. I feel like I need a great deal of flexibility and control over my schedule, and it has to be very part time and predictable. And I want to be really good at what I do, and confident. That's a lot to ask for when one is starting out new. I'm finally doing quite well at home. I have a sense of confidence and efficacy as a mother and homemaker.

And yet I feel a tiny pushing for more—like a tendril sprout, nothing large or mighty. I like writing and it seems to feed me, not drain me the way some other work could do. Writing actually contributes toward my recovery and it's totally flexible—fitting nicely around my unpredictable energy level and my children. I was thinking it might be a way I could use some of the professional knowledge I already have too, instead of starting all over trying to learn a new profession. But I don't know.

I'm going to take this rehab process very slowly, living the question with all the patience and hope I can muster. And reminding myself to be lovingly curious about my responses to what comes up. I think that's the only way I'll endure it without collapsing in self-doubt and criticism. In any event, you won't be seeing my name on those magazine articles when you're standing in the checkout line at the grocery store. I don't plan to write about diets, fashion fads, and sexual techniques. That's one thing I can tell you for sure.

E-MAIL: TO CHRISTIN
DATE: FEBRUARY 8, 2002

Hello to you sweet Christin:

Yesterday a terrific blizzard with stinging sleet left sheets of ice covering all the meadows, and I couldn't let the animals out of the barn because the footing was treacherous. Naisa becomes entirely cranky in the winter and starts to go crazy with cabin fever. She butts everything, even her own food bales. I think when the previous owners removed her horn buds she was partially lobotomized. Goats' brains are right under their horns; there are no sinuses. In winter, Naisa becomes desperate. I don't think she realizes that spring will come.

I wanted to tell you about an interesting conversation I had with Benjamin last week when he was supposed to write a "response to literature" piece—an essay giving his personal reaction to a story, rather than simply retelling it. The story was Pearl Buck's "The Old Demon," where Mrs. Wang opens the sluice to stop the Japanese army, aware she too will drown. After several drafts, Benjamin was still struggling with the assignment. So his teacher gave him a more specific task: answering the question "Was Mrs. Wang brave?" That produced a one-word essay: "Yes."

He came home from school utterly perplexed. "I just can't do this, Mom. I don't know how to explain 'brave.'" He continued, "If you are from another land and you speak a different language, I could explain it to you, because you may not know what the word means. But if you already know what the word means, it is pointless for me to explain how Mrs. Wang is brave. It's not something to explain, like how a car runs. You just have to read the story, and if the author does a good job, you figure it out for yourself."

Somehow we managed to get through the assignment, and I once again mused how his struggles with writing and especially with abstract thought—a typical developmental challenge for children his age—so paralleled my own difficulties after the accident. And I wondered what I would write about bravery if asked to do so. I think that going to school every day is an act of bravery for children with learning disabilities. My friend Gretchen and Michael's terminally ill patients are brave because they get out of bed each morning. Anyone who chooses to remain hopeful in the face of despair is showing great courage.

Flipping through one of the books you recommended, I recently discovered a poet I like. William Carlos Williams was a pediatrician who started writing his poems on prescription pads between appointments; perhaps he too was inspired by patients. I tracked down an old book at the Brick House Book Shop for Michael's birthday; he's forty-five now. I really like Williams' wheelbarrow poem, and there are several about winter and one about a black-eyed susan flower. Really short, just little pieces about life, noted between patients. We read a bunch of them while eating birthday cake.

Later that night, after I thought everyone was asleep, I heard noises in Ekta's room and went to check on her. She was wide awake and so excited. She told me she had just written her first poem.

"I was lying here kind of sleeping and it came right into my head, Mom, so I wrote it down." She pulled her flashlight out from under her pillow and opened her notebook. Precious Ekta, who has not yet been able to master reading or writing, but does have a journal that she keeps by her bed, because that's what her friends do. She opened to a page and showed me her first-ever journal writing.

"Would you like me to read it?" I asked her. She was beaming, so excited she could hardly sit still beside me. I read out loud:

You must be seated by Ekta at Jan. 28, 2002 9:00 to 9:20

As you rest comefertbely in your chair, you might be reading a book or the newspaper, and you would reech your hand down

to the floor and you might cetch a dream and holed it gently like a childs hand and even thogh the dream is quick you shell

holed on and never let go.

—Ekta Sampson

"Oh Ekta, I love your poem."

"Do you, Mom? Really, is it exactly right?"

"Oh yes, it's even more than exactly right."

She was bouncing up and down. "Is every word right too? I mean the spelling, because I think I'm going to show it to my friend Jenna tomorrow, and I want the spelling to be right on every word." So I asked her if she'd like me to type it up and print it out on the computer. She wanted two copies—one for Daddy to take to work.

After school the next day, she told me that her teacher read her poem to the class. I asked her how that felt. She said, "It felt like my face was turning red but it felt good, too."

E-MAIL: TO CHRISTIN
DATE: FEBRUARY 13, 2002

Dear Christin,

You always give me such peace of mind when I start getting twisted up around these writing questions. I'll say more about that later because I have been doing some thinking. But now I just wanted to thank you for your offer to help. And then I have to go sleep before I collect my children from school.

The house smells like nutmeg and ginger, maybe cinnamon, too. I baked cookies for Valentine's Day. We'll decorate them tonight with the Girl Scouts and give them to the Meals on Wheels people tomorrow for delivery to shut-ins.

I had another appointment at vocational rehab, this time with a computer that asked me a million questions about whether I'd like to make kitchen cabinets, guard money in an armored car, conduct a symphony, teach people how to exercise, and a few other imaginative pursuits. Michael told me he took one of those inventories in high school and his printout suggested he should be a farmer or a truck driver. Oh well. Maybe the technology has improved in the past thirty years. If not, perhaps I'll be a bowling alley attendant. In the meantime, I'm a tired mother on my way to bed.

Much love. And Happy Valentine's Day!

Hello to you, dearest Christin, on this snowy March morning,

Wednesday after town meeting day, the kids return to school in happy spirits. We always get an extra couple days of winter vacation because the school buildings are used for town meeting and voting. I think Vermont may be the only state that holds real town meetings anymore; we often have curious tourist types stopping in to see democracy at work.

Ekta said this morning that she's ready for warm weather and grass, but I'm afraid we've got a while to wait. At least the hens have started laying and there are sap buckets on the trees. The roads are still frozen most days, but occasionally they thaw enough so that your feet squish up air bubbles in the mud. And the children carve rivulets from one puddle to the next as we go walking with Bravo and our shovels. Benjamin says that's his favorite thing about mud season— the road construction. At thirteen, he still fancies springtime puddles and idly draws one path after another to drain water this way or that.

Your last letter reminded me how far ahead of ours your Oregon spring arrives. And I've kept your sentence in my head, the one about writing, and how goal-orientation seems to kill creative spirit. You said the writing has to be "like the warm breeze over the pasture that melts the ice and teases the trees into releasing their spring buds." I like that sentence; I love that time of year. It's coming. Not yet, but soon.

I got that book you had mentioned, picked it up when we went to Burlington for the flower show. We go every year during the February break. Benjamin belongs to the Garden Railroad Society; they set up a train that travels through hundreds of daffodils and tulips buried in mounds of mulch. He's the only member under sixty years old, I think, and it's fun to see him tinkering around the tracks with his senior cronies.

Anyway, I've been reading the essays on and off for about a week now, and I'm struggling. I decided to finish them because it would be good practice—an academic exercise—but honestly, I don't think I understand very much. I was actually surprised by how little I manage to glean. And it brings me to the humbling truth that I am basically a very simple-minded creature now. I don't dance well with complex concepts and philosophies anymore. And surely dear Christin, if you think I can digest those essays, you are overestimating my intelligence! I can't chew up those huge heady topics any better than two week-old French bread.

Ah well, maybe it will get easier, and maybe once I finish the book I'll understand more. We'll see. In any event, I do recall that you thought it would help to keep me focused on writing for art's sake rather than writing for publication. I think perhaps it might, but like I said, I don't understand very much so it's hard to tell.

In the meantime, I'm doing a lot of organizing: keys, mittens, coats, skates, school papers, cassette tapes, sheet music, flower vases, medicines, photographs, tea leaves, candles, catalogues, bed linens, and boots. All of our drawers and closets need a major overhaul, and that requires those "executive functions" that challenge me. So it is good work. It is also helping me to see the concrete stuff that my life is made of. When I contemplate writing, I am acutely aware that I can only write about what I know. And what I know is very mundane indeed. But that's OK because there are probably a few other people who might find it refreshing to read about the mundane. As a psychotherapist and a mother (not a historian or literary artist), I must admit I actually like the personal and psychological stuff. It's what I know, where I'm comfortable. But I do see where it could lead to sentimental navel-gazing. I would hope to avoid that. So in any event, I've been trying to organize my journal notes and letters along with all the closets and drawers.

You mentioned that you didn't want to let the cat in because he might send an e-mail again. I solved the problem of interfering paws on my own keyboard by putting a spare office chair right next to mine, with an inviting blanket on it. Now the kitties curl up asleep beside me rather than trying to bounce all over my fingers while I am typing. Perhaps an extra chair by your computer would keep your cat out of trouble?

Much much love.

E-mail: To Christin
Date: March 13, 2002

Good morning sweet Christin,

Actually it's lunchtime, but that's still morning where you are. I know because I just called a hotel on the Pacific Ocean, and the receptionist said "Good morning." We're going to take a trip to La Jolla, California during the last week of April. Michael wants to see the ocean. Benjamin wants to see Legoland. Ekta wants to see Afghanistan; it's so like her to want to go directly into the center of pain she can't comprehend. Benjamin suggested that we avoid any destination engaged in military action, so she settled for polar bears at the San Diego Zoo. I'm hoping to see acres of wildflowers before they all turn into parking lots.

The receptionist took our reservation and ended the call by explaining that she could not confirm the bedding for our room. Although we need two double beds for the four of us, they won't guarantee a room with two double beds unless we pay an extra two hundred dollars! We'll just have to take our chances, and that means we may get a room with one king-size bed. In which case I guess we'll all turn sideways and sleep with our feet sticking out.

I realize I probably shouldn't try to write to you on Wednesday mornings, because I'm so groggy from my late night Tuesdays. I'm taking a fourteen-week master gardening course that keeps me out until ten p.m. Ugh! I thought it might be time to try something that would stretch me just one night a week. I'm five weeks into it and regretting that decision. But I'll stick it out and just remember that I'm not ready for this type of schedule yet. By the way, those fruit trees you planted sound lovely, and do you know about putting out bars of strong-smelling soap to keep the deer away? Simply tie it to the branches. I do it every year; Irish Spring is what my gardens smell like for several weeks.

The FedEx man just arrived at the door, so now I have to play dress-up. Not with him, but with my new clothes. I'm supposed to be in a concert with Ekta this Friday, and concert dress means black and elegant—neither of which is hanging in my closet. I just realized that on Sunday. Thank goodness for catalogues and mail order. Hopefully something will fit. Then I'll have to figure out how to stuff my feet into those pinching shiny patent pumps that I've never liked. Or perhaps I could just paint the nail on my big toe with a green marker. Then I could wear my cute and cozy canvas China shoes with the rose embroidery that's missing a green leaf because of the hole I've worn through.

I wish I could write more now, but I'm on a schedule to get in two hours of sleep before I head off. Anyway, I just wanted you to have a cheery hello.

Beauty

14

Peepers' Song

Journal: April 6, 2002

Six-thirty on a Saturday morning. Michael is off to work out; Benjin and Ekta still sleeping. I'm feeling quite well rested and happy this morning. Sun is bright, birds are singing. The snow is mostly gone from the valleys, though temperatures are frigid and sap is running. This is the day before we spring the clocks forward, so I'm enjoying the feeling of being alert this early in the day, kind of an hour ahead of things, knowing it will change tomorrow.

Benjamin has not yet trotted down the hallway and pounced upon me with his bright-eyed good morning, a light kiss on my cheek, and the ritual question, "Can I go on the computer?" This is a nice change, for me to be awake before he is and to see him snuggled into his covers sound asleep, with the sunlight streaming in upon him.

He told me the other day that he wants black curtains. "I hate the light," he said. I was draping black silk over his windows as he was climbing into bed.

"Benjamin, how could anybody hate the light?"

"I don't really hate the light; I just hate waking up in it. This time of year, the sun pours in on you before you even have a chance to open your eyes. It's so much better to wake up in darkness. That's why I like winter."

I said maybe we could ask Minnow to make him some curtains out of that black fabric with the roosters on it. She just finished Ekta's lovely purple curtains with bed pillows to match.

I peeked in at Ekta this morning too, wrapped up in lavender on the little bed she's soon to outgrow. And I thought what a precious time of life this is, this "time between" when our children are still with us, not off on their own pursuits, but independent enough not to be so demanding of our physical energy. How greatly I enjoy being with them, and I know it can't last forever. Now, finally, I have a perspective of time I couldn't have had when they were babies. Now, too, understanding how quickly it all passes, I want to savor it deeply, because all too soon the sunlight will be streaming in on empty beds, except for holidays or summer visits.

I was thinking too, as Michael drove off to his weight lifting, about this midlife time to enjoy being healthy and fit, with muscles, bones, and lungs still strong enough to skate like he does—playing hockey with the twenty-five year-olds who can't possibly appreciate their youthful bodies the way a forty-five year-old can. Life is good here at the midlife threshold, this time between youth and old age.

Last night I celebrated no snow in the yard (though the pond is still frozen) by wearing my purple rubber clogs down to the barn. Felt pretty spiffy walking along the garden paths down to the meadow. But I regretted my decision when I had to run after Bravo, catching his mane to convince him to go into the barn. He was having his own springtime romp in the meadow with no intention of curtailing his fun for me. The clogs stayed on my feet at least, but I think I'll revert to barn boots today. Guess I should head down and let the critters out now, since the children are still sleeping.

And then I want to get to my book. I wonder if it will turn into anything, or if I won't be able to make much sense of these pages. I look back over my journal and correspondence with Christin and much of it seems redundant to me now: so often I'm tired, on my way to a nap, or just emerging from a period of fatigue. And every other time, it seems, I'm dealing with the loss of self, grieving over who I am no longer, and trying to figure out who I will be when I'm done with all this.

One day last week, I was just lying down for a nap when Barli called. She asked if I still sleep every afternoon. When I said that I do nap almost every day, she sounded surprised, as if she assumed that I carried on like everyone else now. She said, "Wow!" with a tone of envy that made me realize how luxurious my lifestyle must sound to her.

I jumped in to say there was a time I thought of it as a luxury too. "As a mother of busy toddlers, napping would have seemed like absolute heaven to me. And now here I am doing just that, and wishing I didn't have to. Isn't that crazy?"

We both laughed. We spend our lives waiting for what we don't have; then, when we have it, we start longing for what we used to have. It's important not to spend too much of one's life waiting, I think.

So I agreed to enjoy my nap, and she her busy afternoon keeping up with her little ones.

I have wanted to write since the moment I received your last e-mail; your journal page was such a joy to read! I'm hoping you are starting to feel more content with the journey of these "sixties" days and your life as a writer. Spring is a fine time of year for new wondering about old questions. I don't know anything about being sixty, of course. But I do know that some days are better than others for existential questions.

Our bluebirds and swallows arrived today. The great blue heron showed up last week, just about the time the crocuses turned up their sweet faces. Our snow is gone early this year. Temperatures are still cold, but the wetlands are blue once again. Hurray! And Bravo is rolling in the sun-drenched straw of his paddock while Naisa frolics in the meadow. She appears to be rehearsing for one of those springtime scenes in Disney's *Bambi*, when all the young ones leap and bound in so many directions at once. I actually wondered yesterday if a bee had stung her, but there are no bees this early, no insects at all, really. She's just happy.

Did I ever tell you that my vocational rehab results are in? And according to all the data I'm supposed to be—not an astronaut, figure skater, bowling alley attendant, or architect. Out of the many thousands of possibilities, my number one profession that matched all criteria was "counseling psychologist." Carol, my voc rehab counselor, was delighted that the software could so accurately synthesize all the data collected and make an appropriate match.

I guess I can see her point. But I wasn't doing all this to discover that the profession for which I am most suited and naturally drawn towards is the one that I used to have. That's not really the information I was looking for. Although just now as I type that sentence I'm wondering what exactly I *was* looking for. Anyway, it's kind of humorous.

Of course the database doesn't get into whether you are able to *do* that profession, just whether you would like it if you were able to do it. So I'm not sure where I'm heading, but it doesn't seem to matter a whole lot right now. Not like it used to, or might again sometime in the future. You know how these things can creep up out of nowhere and suddenly pull you off center.

Funny thing: yesterday Benjamin was working on a questionnaire for a social studies project and one of the questions was about work. How many hours a week does your dad work, and your mom. So he figured Michael probably works about seventy hours a week. Then he said, "You don't do any work do you, Mom?"

I protested, "What do you mean? Seems to me like I'm working all the time." I was teasing, but he was concerned about my feelings and quickly added, "Not a real job, not like you used to have."

I said, "That's true. But I'm writing a book."

"Yeah, but that's not real work, like a job," he said.

Ah, so interesting, I thought. And isn't this the same pesky monster that's recently been nipping at your ankles, dear Christin? And mine too, a little, on gray days when I'm tired and feeling quite bored with the pages of my simple book.

On other days, bright warm days that invite me out to the wildflower meadow, I'm very happy that I don't work at a "real job." I think perhaps the best work is to adore this marvelous creation, to soak up all the blessing of simply being alive. To witness the splendid miracle of every moment. Then I have to laugh at myself and think how goofy I sound. At least your Mother Ann at the convent could speak with some sort of spiritual authority on that point of "living only to praise." I sound like a crazy person when I start saying things like that. Besides, that idea really only works for some people, lucky people who can walk outside in the springtime and count baby lupine leaves coming up in the wildflower meadow. It doesn't work for the millions of unlucky people trying to keep their families alive in bleak landscapes where children starve and teenagers turn themselves into bombs.

And then, dear Christin, I can't bear to go any further with the conversation in my head. So like my sprite, wee Naisa, I kick up my heels this way and that and dash about. Off to play a concert at the nursing home, then to Girl Scouts to plan the fishing campout, then to drama rehearsal to help the kids choreograph a dance and to the craft store to pick up clay for Benjamin's science project. Then dinner, homework, and laundry. That's pretty much all I can think about, and most of the time that's quite enough.

Amazing, isn't it, how you can have such a glorious morning—like the day the deer waited for you to walk your soul out of bed. Where does it come from? And why don't we realize it's right here for us now, every moment?

But I do like what you said: "What does it matter whether or not the word is read by anyone, since it is being; it is what we are." I like being what you call a "peon of praise." In fact I'm going to adopt that as my new job title. Perhaps if that one had been in the vocational database, it might have been the precise profession to match my every criteria right now.

Anyway, dear one, I must go rest. I do so much love your journaling. I am happy that you have not stopped writing altogether. And always I send much love.

I have been thinking about your Irish Spring garden and hoping the skunks have decided they'd prefer a different scent. I realized I never told you about some other alternatives that might help deter the deer. There's an organic material called Milorganite. It's made of human waste, so the deer don't like to come anywhere close. I haven't actually used it, because the soap works just fine for my garden. But I don't have a lot of skunks around either. Now the interesting thing is that it's from Milwaukee; for some reason urine from Wisconsin males seems to do the trick. I thought that since Michael's from close to Wisconsin, maybe he could just pee around the gardens before going to sleep. And of course John, being a Minnesota boy himself, might very well try the same thing—you know, kind of a territorial marking. Maybe it would work for skunks.

The gardens here are starting to burst. We've had two days of record-breaking heat, like eighty-five and eighty-eight degrees—really high temperatures even for summer, much less April. Michael and the kids actually went into the pond last night. And it seems the ice barely left there last week! The thermometer at the bank said ninety when I passed by this afternoon. There is still snow at Benjamin's school, and Michael said people are skiing up on the mountain. He just fixed a broken arm and the boy was totally sunburned. I think the only thing he was wearing were goggles.

Down here in the valley the peepers are in full chorus, and Benjamin sleeps with earplugs now. The "frog run" is over. That's the last run of sap for the season; they call it that because it usually happens just about the time the frogs start to sing. In fact they started singing the night Ekta had her last concert. We came home late and stepped out into the clear starry night and there it was, the sound that makes my heart smile, rising up faintly out of the wetlands, the song that tells me winter's gone away. Today my forsythia is coming into bloom, and I'm hoping not to miss all the tulips and daffodils that seem to have appeared almost overnight.

We're leaving for San Diego on Saturday, and if the weather continues like this, everything will bloom while we're away. Of course right now I'm thinking I'd rather not be leaving home. But usually we still have plenty of snow this time of year and a long while until the flower fairies get busy with their springtime palettes. This is so unusual, and very sweet—these temperatures, with no bugs and no weeds. The yellowbirds haven't even made it back yet; they're usually the first heralds of winter's end.

In any event, right now I've got much to do to prepare for our trip. We'll be gone until next Saturday in LaJolla, California where, ironically, the temperature will probably be cooler than in Vermont. Mostly I just wanted to check in with you to see how you are doing these days. Because I think you have been quiet for some time now. Is that true, or is it just my warped sense of time? I do hope you are happy. Please be well there where you are, dear Christin. May the wildflowers bloom on your land. My love goes with you always.

E-MAIL: TO CHRISTIN
DATE: APRIL 29, 2002

I received your latest wonderful e-mail just before leaving for San Diego. Right before our earthquake, in fact. The whole house shook and rattled for what seemed like two minutes, but the official report was that it lasted only about thirty seconds. I've never experienced an earthquake before; it's not something that often happens in Vermont.

That was after our three record-breaking, ninety-degree days. And then a night of spectacular northern lights and coyotes howling. Then spring came to a screeching halt. Even the peepers went back to bed, and all is now silent under snow once again.

Oh well. All these droopy daffodils remind me it will come again. And we didn't miss a thing by going to California. Our trip was just right. We didn't have the warmest of temperatures, but sunny and altogether quite pleasant. The place we stayed was right on the Pacific with a private sandy beach. It was as comfortable and beautifully landscaped as I'd hoped it would be, just perfect. Legoland, the zoo, aquarium, and breeding programs at the wild animal park met all expectations; no one was disappointed. The fields full of ranunculus were glorious, and we also saw Cirque du Soleil, that amazing troupe of acrobats and dancers from around the globe.

While we were off gallivanting, a rat moved into the barn. Most likely he's been there all winter, and that explains the missing eggs and bits of broken eggshells. It might also explain Pepperpot's bloody feet and why she insists on roosting in the rafters now. I wonder if he tried to carry her off to his hole one night. Our caretaker told us she saw the rat under the hay that had collected beneath the stairs. She cleared it out while we were away, and yesterday Michael put rat poison down the holes. I suspect we'll go down there some morning and stumble over the corpse. Each of us is hoping somebody else gets that dubious honor.

I was delighted to read that you've started to work on your "Gypsy Bones" manuscript again. And I'm curious about the rewrite; how is it going? I am really starting to understand a bit about the importance of finding the right structure for the work. What a bugaboo that can create!

And switching topics briefly—to garden structure: Before I forget, regarding that feast you're laying out for the deer each night, I'm going to send you some recommendations for alternative plants. It sounds as though you have made your garden entirely too appetizing and you need to add a few liver and onion-type entrees. Don't worry about your lupine. It will come right back, grow new leaves, and bloom just a little later, which will be a nice surprise for you—lupine in the summer.

That brings me back to this question of structure, so essential to both gardens and writing. I still have not figured out how to proceed with structuring my book, but right now I'm going to make egg salad and then practice the French horn, so that I can be ready to play in Ekta's concert. Fortunately, I have a mouthpiece. When I decided to bring it along to keep my lip muscles in shape during our vacation, it never occurred to me that I'd set off the alarm at the San Diego airport. Luckily, it wasn't confiscated.

In any event, it's good to be home, in our snow-dappled, greening fields, and to deal with small questions, like structural issues for books and deer-safe gardens, rather than great ones like breeding giant pandas or miniature sea horses.

I'll write more tomorrow. Always my love.

15

Cake and Lemonade

E-mail: To Christin
Date: May 17, 2002

I can't believe it's taken this long to get back to you, but here it is Friday again. Last Friday was Ekta's performance. She was the rose seller in the play *Oliver*, and how sweetly she sang her solo. I'm barely just now recovering from the whirlwind of rehearsals and shopping trips for props and costume supplies. And there were three performances. This past week I have mostly been trying to get on my feet again.

This is an odd time of day to be writing. Usually I write in the morning, once I've gotten the children settled into school and taken care of the barn chores, but all week I've been going back to bed in the morning and still need to sleep again in the afternoon. So I've not done any writing, and not much else either.

Now I'm remembering that I told myself I'm not going to talk to you any more about how much I have to sleep. That has become a very tedious topic indeed. So please kindly scratch the above paragraph.

Our weather has been terribly un-May-like. I can't believe I was worried about missing the tulips by going to San Diego; they still haven't opened. We even had snow here this past week.

In any event, it's dinnertime on Friday and I'm alone, because Michael and Ekta have gone off on a "date" to pick up Chinese food and rent a movie. Benjamin is at a sleepover in Montpelier with classmates from his old school. They're gathering at the gold-domed State House, where they'll take turns playing Frisbee on the capitol lawn and standing in line to buy tickets for the new *Star Wars* movie. Sounds like real teenager stuff to me. Shadow, Benjamin's kitty, is sulking. When he didn't come home from school with the rest of us as usual, she went up to his bedroom, curled up in his bed, and hasn't budged.

I'll write more soon—the nice kind of "morning with a friend" writing that I prefer to do—as soon as my mornings are back to normal. You are always in my heart.

Journal: May 24, 2002

What an unusual spring it's been, with that record-breaking streak of ninety-plus temperatures back in April when snow was still on the ground, then the earthquake, followed by the gloomy weeks of May. One morning Ekta told me she couldn't bear the gray sky any longer. She said it was weighing down so heavily that it made her eyebrows ache.

Finally today the sun is shining and I'm sitting in my chaise on the porch, just finishing a lunch of chicken salad, which Mr. Crazy Moon, the cat, was far too eager to help me polish off. If it hadn't been for that three-foot snake he delivered proudly to our doorstep this morning, I might have gladly shared my lunch. But after watching him sink his teeth into those reptilian guts, I thought better of welcoming him to my plate. For dessert I'll have my last piece of birthday cake—the cake that created so much trouble.

Bravo is whinnying enthusiastically from the paddock. At first I thought he was greeting me, anticipating the moment I'd step off the porch and head down to lead him into green grass. But I realized he hadn't even noticed me; his attention was fixed on the pond, where two geese were battling each other with their broad wings. There is a childless pair and a couple with just one fuzzy gosling between them. Unusual. I wonder if the cold affected their fertility this year.

The hillsides have never looked so odd. That hot streak in April forced the early-budding trees into their springtime green color, but then everything stopped and remained stuck like that for the next month. There was this odd green color splotched around the mountainsides amidst lots of gray and brown and dark wintergreen. Next came the red—plenty of red all over—from buds waiting for sunshine to bring out their chlorophyll. It was kind of an autumn-looking panorama: not a Vermont autumn, but a someplace autumn. Then snow fell and covered the higher elevations, and everything really did look completely strange.

So far there are few babies of any kind—ducks, geese, turtles. I'm grateful today for the sun and for the gusting breezes that ring my chimes from tree to tree.

E-MAIL: TO CHRISTIN
DATE: MAY 25, 2002

Sweet Christin,

I've been to the barn and back in my nightgown this morning. For the first time in weeks we're having sunshine and a temperature above forty degrees. Michael drove the children to school, so I took a leisurely stroll through the barn chores, enjoying the smells this warmer temperature evokes.

My birthday was quite wonderful. Gloomy outside but not wet, so we did a little yard work. We're trying to overhaul the vegetable/railroad garden so the radishes don't grow over the tracks this year. The guys have an idea to build a mountain with a tunnel through it, which means finding a new place for Ekta's sweet peas.

I was resting on the couch when they brought me a gift: two pairs of garden gloves in big sizes, one for Michael and one for Benjamin. Assuming the promise that accompanies the gesture, I was quite pleased. They also gave me a laundry basket that they intend to use themselves—another great idea! For dinner they cooked up a springtime omelet with asparagus and mushrooms and a cake decorated with M&M's and little bear candles. Ekta was quite upset about the cake, because she had it all planned out to be a double layer cake baked in two heart-shaped pans and decorated with fresh flowers in water picks. But when she and Michael went off to the grocery store for supplies she never detailed her plans to him. Nor had he seen the intricate diagrams she had sketched in her notebook.

She was still sleeping the next morning when he rose early to bake the cake before we left for church. He baked it in a bundt pan. Ekta didn't see it until right before dinnertime, when he brought it out of hiding for her to decorate. She was furious. They made me stay out in the garden until dinner was ready, so I came into the middle of a big squabble. Throughout the meal I was trying to figure out why everyone was so tense. Finally, when the cake was delivered, Ekta could no longer contain her disappointment. And my compliments failed to restore congenial feelings.

By bedtime, though, all ruffled feathers had been smoothed. Ekta said she hadn't wanted to discuss it at dinner in front of Dad because "his feelings were probably hurt since he thought he had done a nice thing by baking the cake." I agreed that might be true. She quickly protested that "he really should have checked out that idea with me first, because it was all the wrong thing. And now you don't have that beautiful double-decker heart cake with all the flowers."

"That's true," I said, "but I have something even better."

"What?" She muttered the word beneath her fierce scowl.

"You."

I was thinking about how one's expectations really do color subjective experience. Not just with birthday cake, but with healing too. It's important to strike a balance between maintaining a degree of hopeful optimism and having realistic expectations. That's a tricky thing, though. Dr. Drudge explained why setting goals for recovery from brain injury is especially difficult: The network is complex, and because you're dealing with a moving target it's simply impossible to know what to expect.

Journal: May 2002

Before my accident I never realized how pervasive a communication disorder can be. It's not simply about finding words, producing sounds, and enunciating. It also can encompass the entire realm of verbal processing and all it impacts in the cognitive domain. That's huge. I wish more people—especially medical professionals—better understood the extent to which thinking of any sort relies on a verbal process.

When Dr. Drudge first referred me to a speech and language pathologist, I was skeptical. I didn't want somebody teaching me how to talk—I wanted to learn how to *think* again. Looking back now, I see how lucky I was to have been referred to a language therapist, because that's what thinking is: verbal, spatial, mathematical—it's all language.

Helen's mother recently had a stroke. She had no physical-muscular impairments, though her communicative functions were severely diminished. After a short hospital stay she was discharged, but her discharge plan didn't include any speech and language therapy. Helen was simply directed to find a live-in companion for her mother and was told that visiting nurses would check on her.

"Unbelievable!" I exclaimed to Michael after speaking with Helen.

"There are still lots of people who just don't get it," he replied, "people in medicine who'll make all kinds of arrangements for the stroke patient with an arm that doesn't move, but they'll send Helen's mom home with no thought to how difficult—impossible, actually—it will be for her to navigate safely through her day without being able to converse, read, or write."

As it turned out—fortunately for Helen's mom—she had a mild complication which required readmission, this time at a different hospital with her own primary care physician looking after her. Due to his good judgment about the impact of her language deficits, she was discharged to a rehab center before returning home. Helen told me that before the stroke her mother was an independent, active, keenly intelligent woman who lived alone in her own home. "She's not herself anymore. She can't read and conversing is difficult; it's hard for her to answer questions."

Helen said that sitting with her mom now was reminding her of our times together after my accident. "I was such a terrible friend," she said.

"No, Helen, you really were the best," I objected.

"But I didn't do anything."

"You did so much, just by being with me," I told her. "Making time to spend with me. Being patient. Treating me like I was still me and not a stupid bore. And remember the carrot-ginger soup you made? That was the greatest thing. When there was no language in my head, the taste of that soup was so comforting, reminding me of my friend named Helen, the one who makes carrot soup." By the time we hung up, Helen was planning to call the minister and see if somebody from church would bring in her mom's favorite milkshake every couple of days.

Food and fragrance are powerful that way, taking you immediately to a place you thought was lost. I remember hearing about a man who'd had a favorite apple tree along the road he walked home from school as a young boy. He decided to graft it so he could have those same sweet apples later in his life. Now, at ninety-one, he could pick an apple from his tree, close his eyes, and with just one bite he is once again that young schoolboy on his way home.

Sense memories don't seem to rely on words to define experience. Perhaps that's why they are nourishing to those of us impaired by language deficits. That also must be why animals are such a blessing: The companionship they provide does not require language. I'm remembering early in my recovery what a relief it was to spend time at the barn—feeding, brushing, and shoveling in silence. I was ever grateful for basic, routine tasks and simple company; no words required with my furry and feathered friends.

When Helen's mom returned home after her stroke she found two motherless kittens who required regular milk feedings. Nothing could have been better for her spirit! When we feel as though we are the ones needing all the help from others, what a gift it is to have an animal that we're actually capable of caring for—an opportunity for nurturing and companionship without language.

E-MAIL: TO CHRISTIN
DATE: MAY 29, 2002

Hello lovely Christin,

I've started wondering if the "new learning" center of my brain will forever function as it does now—not very well—or if it may improve with use. I think that's one of the reasons I took that horticulture course, a little experiment in new learning. We'll see. If it can't improve much, that's OK. I have enough strategies to accommodate for it relatively well. It's just interesting to realize how I used to be able to learn practically anything almost instantly and then have the information readily available to me without needing to refer to notes or texts. And now I have to reread many times— slowly, arduously—to recall something. I don't mind, really; I know that's how I work now so I generally plan for it and rely on my strategies.

I recently sent a card to a friend who is recovering from surgery, and I think I said something like, "Try to enjoy this time, this slower-paced healing time." And as I was writing I realized that my slower-paced healing time is over. The calendar is filling up with activities and events that I'm solely responsible for handling. The pace has quickened. I'm not fast, but I'm definitely somewhere in that wide spectrum of "normal." And that means busy again, busy like everybody else. I'm not saying that's necessarily a desirable goal, but simply observing that I'm no longer feeling left out of the action. Now there are moments when I need to remind myself, *Relax. You are in the right place at the right time. Remember to enjoy it.*

Another thing that is clearly different for me now is that I have an analytical, judging faculty in operation once again. I realized the other day that I'm starting to become more opinionated. For such a long, long time after the injury I experienced most things with incredibly blank neutrality. I think there is a sort of emotional apathy that comes with loss and grieving. But my indifference was prolonged and persistent, even when I could honestly describe myself as content, grateful, even happy. I realize now that it probably came from my diminished processing ability. Since it took nearly all of my faculties just to understand what was happening or being said around me, I had no ability to analyze, evaluate, and produce an opinion about it. But that's changing now—not in a huge way, but enough that I startled myself a few days ago with a rather uncharitable thought about what someone was saying to me.

Of course one of the gifts of this injury is that the experience itself is humbling, but this new insight goes beyond simple humility. It grows out of my "not-thinking" experience of life, from a time in my recovery when formulating thoughts was impossible and what I had instead was neutrality on things that I would have once cared about quite intensely. I hope I will be able to hold onto this—not as indifference, but as neutrality. There is a clarity that comes from it. We see farther. I want to remember that, now that my mind is speeding up and neutrality is harder to maintain.

Actually, there is quite a bit I want to remember. That must be the real motivation now behind my book. It's like something you said in your e-mail—about how a good story doesn't simply tell what's happened. You wrote,

> It communicates a movement of the spirit, a longing, a leaning and yearning towards a denouement, towards a clarification. So the story is always looking forwards, not backwards. Even a memoir is written as an author's search for clarification and not as an attempt to teach, explain, justify, etc. My guess is that this is what distinguishes the good memoirs from those we never finish reading.

That makes a lot of sense to me as I piece together this book, remembering things I've learned and don't ever want to lose, unexpected gifts I could not have imagined but am grateful to have received.

We had a quiet Memorial Day. Michael was working; Ekta and I were organizing her things and packing up for her class trip to Camp Keewaydin. Benjamin hauled our bikes out of their winter storage at the barn and tuned them up so we could bike down to Snow's Creamy stand. As it turned out, we decided to take a different route, avoiding holiday traffic on the paved roads. We headed off through the pastures and wound our way along the dandelion-yellow meadows spotted with black and white cows.

Right past the intersection at the big barn we came upon a red wagon with a cardboard sign: "Lemonade For Sale." Just up the road, two little boys ran out of their kitchen door. "Lemonade! Five cents!" they called to us from behind their fence, waving their arms and jumping up and down. "Do you want some lemonade?" But I didn't have any money; it was home on my bed, in the pocket of the shorts I'd just changed out of.

"I'd love some lemonade," I called back to them, slowing my pedaling, "but I don't have any money. We'll come back some other time to buy your lemonade."

The younger brother didn't hear me. He kept jumping up and down saying, "Lemonade—five cents," but the older boy ran toward the house. "MOM, M-O-M!!" I heard him calling as I continued up the road. "They're coming back. They're gonna get some money. And they're coming back. We're gonna sell some lemonade!"

I knew they couldn't have too many customers out there, between the cows and the mountains. As I pedaled away I would have given just about anything for a nickel in my pocket. Then I saw it: a shiny silver buffalo in the gravel at the road's edge. Good angels we have! I circled back and picked it up.

"Looks like our lucky day!" I called to Benjin and Ekta, and we headed back to the lemonade stand.

My last time biking on that road was September 12. We have a different world now—smaller, I think, and more fragile. Life is precious; so is peace. Five-cent lemonade offered to you by muddy-faced, widely grinning, barefooted and barebottomed entrepreneurs is not something to pass up.

At bedtime Ekta said, "Mom let's have a moment of silence for all the people who have died." And we did.

Joy

16

Confidence

Happy Tuesday in June to you, sweet Christin,

How is your summer going? And your writing and your gardens? Thank God you are not dealing with fires this year, like so much of the West. We are deluged with showers and flood warnings regularly. How I wish some of it could blow west, but it never seems to.

Today is the second day of soccer camp and I'm realizing it is now fully two years that we've been at this writing together you and I, this weaving of my mind back together again. In one of your earliest e-mails you wrote: "I'm so honored that you would entrust your self to this correspondence with me, and that together we can find that part of you that became a 'stranger' as you describe. It's okay to cuddle up next to each other here. To hold each other in our words, in our souls."

I just wanted to say thank you for your never-ending love and for weaving your beautiful words around my heart and soul these many long months. I cherish your letters as I cherish you. And I wanted to celebrate our writing anniversary by letting my fingers walk around this keyboard like they used to do for hours at a time. Then, I struggled so to make thoughts out of impulses; translating them into words was such labor. Now I have many things to write, if only I had the opportunity to sit still long enough to write them down. Can you believe what I just said? I'm remembering all those tedious hours when the only thing I *could* do was sit still.

In any event, I'll fill you in on what's going on of late. Because we have a lot of summer rituals, I find myself having experiences much like last summer's or the one before—only now I'm much better! It's easy to see my progress, so I'm celebrating many small triumphs.

We went to York, Maine when school let out last week. On the way we picked up my niece Bethany, which was good because Ekta was in a funk about school ending and it gave her something else to think about. It's not so much the ending of school that troubles her but the beginning of sixth grade—going to middle school, a new building, new classes. Apprehensive about next year's teachers, she was relieved to hear that the one she met on step-up day is retiring. When I picked her up from school she said, "Mom, that teacher can read your mind. Imagine how awful that would be!"

It didn't help that Benjamin was jubilant on step-up day, thrilled with his new teacher and classmates. His homeroom teacher is also the soccer coach so Benjin already knows him, and he has good friends in the class. His special educator will move with him to eighth grade, so it looks as though all is in place for a successful start. Now he can relax into summer.

Not so with Ekta. Of course part of it is being eleven and a girl. She gets her stomach in knots worrying about who her special educator will be and whether she'll be able to do sixth grade work, even though her fifth grade report card shows all the highest marks. Knowing she won't have the teacher who can read her thoughts is some consolation, but what will the new teacher be like? A new school is hard work. She just did it last year; now she has to make the transition again.

After step-up day, Ekta told me there was something she wanted to talk to me about—a question she had but it felt too awful to say out loud—and she asked if she could write it down and give it to me. I assured her there could never be anything so awful that we couldn't somehow work it out together. And I said she could ask me her question whatever way would be best for her.

She disappeared to her room and closed the door. Minutes later she placed a torn shred of paper in my hand and said, "Don't read it out loud."

Wondering what in her young life could be so awfully scary, I looked over the penciled words: "What if when I was older somebody said don't make friends with black people?"

This one I was going to have to think about for a while. There were simple answers, like "Tell them that's stupid," or "Tell them it's too bad they think like that because they're going to miss out on a lot of wonderful friends," or "Tell yourself you wouldn't want to be friends with someone who thinks like that."

I did say those words as I hugged her. But there is more, much more to it than that. And I'm white. It is simply not possible for me to know her fear the way that she knows it. I told her that it was a really important question and I'm glad she asked me. And I said I'm going to have to think some more about it.

Well, the trip to York, Maine was short. We spent the summer solstice basking on the sunny beach and then had dinner at Fox's by the Nubble Lighthouse. The girls climbed down on the cliffs to watch some scuba divers engage in their lengthy suiting-up rituals. Bethany took the binoculars so they could focus back on our restaurant table and see when the dinner arrived. That way they'd know when to return. Meanwhile, Benjamin went to check out a seagull that was hanging from the telephone wire. He reported to us that a fishing line had become tangled in the wire after an errant casting off. Evidently the gull went after the fishing bait and became caught, just like a fish might have been if the fisherman had had better luck. Now the utility crew would be called to free the dead bird.

Back at our quaint suite of rooms, upstairs over the Black Dog gift shop, the girls decided to shower together before going to bed. I went into the bathroom to brush my teeth and overheard them comparing their latest physical developments, the things that had changed since last summer. Bethany was taller; Ekta's legs were longer from hipbone to floor. Bethany's breasts were bigger and Ekta said they looked just right—not funny like last year. Ekta had a hint of armpit hair but she didn't smell bad. Bethany had no hair yet, but said her mom tells her all the time that she stinks, so now she has to wear deodorant.

Ekta thought that was pretty lucky, having your own deodorant, but Bethany didn't agree. She offered to let Ekta try it out just to prove her point. Ekta was so eager, she dried off right away. And when Bethany handed over one of her outgrown preteen bras, Ekta remarked admiringly, "I just love having you for a cousin." Bethany explained how she tie-dyed the bra using rubber bands here and there, and produced a pair of underpants to match.

The next day was dreary and rained nonstop so we packed up early and headed home, thankful for our totally perfect beach visit on the longest day of the year. Back in Vermont, we hit a pothole and ended up with a flat tire. There were a few other mishaps to be endured as well, but I think all would agree that one perfect day at the beach was quite worth the effort.

So now they're off at camp. Ekta is doing a Girl Scout day camp at Lake Elmore, her first time opting out of soccer camp. I think it was a good decision. This morning we painted her hair bright green for crazy hair day. I'm happily amazed at how easily this year I'm able to handle the shuttling schedule, which includes two trips a day to Craftsbury along with meeting the Girl Scout bus and ferrying Benjamin to summer hockey in the evening. I was apprehensive, yet so far it seems to be much easier than I remember it being last year. Certainly my energy is stronger than it was twelve months ago.

Yesterday, after I said goodbye to Benjamin at camp, one of the dads came up to me and asked how to take the dirt road shortcut back from Craftsbury. I was pleased to be on the helping side of things this year instead of repeatedly asking for directions. As we walked through the parking lot the man told me that we'd met before. "My wife and I came to you for marriage counseling about four years ago," he said. "I heard about your accident. You may not remember us; it was a long time ago."

I could sort of place him—not perfectly, but it didn't matter. "I'm sorry," I said. "Sometimes I have trouble recognizing people. But thank you for telling me who you are. And how are things going now for your family?"

"Great," he said. "We're fine now, all of us. You really helped us. We didn't see you a lot, but it really helped. We just needed time and patience, like you said."

By then, we had reached our cars. "Yes, time and patience can work miracles," I said. "And commitment, too—that's a pretty big one. I'm glad you're doing well. Thanks for telling me."

I climbed into my car and started driving. I headed down the road in the wrong direction, but realized it soon enough and turned around. It didn't matter; he followed me. And I got it right the second time.

I was full to bursting with the realization that I don't need to go to my office again—or to any office—to retrieve a part of myself that seemed to be lost. I'm not lost.

I like who I'm becoming. Benjamin teases me often, because my words don't always come out quite right. I say a lot of dumb funny things, especially when I'm tired. It's just fine. I don't worry about it anymore. And I know how to plan my days so that I won't make bad mistakes—dangerous ones. I don't worry about that too much either.

I told Benjin today that it's good he teases me. He was surprised. "Why?" he asked. I said it's a great thing when somebody you love helps you laugh at yourself. A sense of humor, especially towards oneself, is a really fine ally.

Just then Ekta came in with only two eggs. "I dropped the third one. It was the weirdest thing," she said rather incredulously. "I was just walking along and thinking in my head about how would it be if I dropped an egg. And I wasn't meaning to do it at all. I was actually just wondering, but all of a sudden it simply fell right through my fingers."

"Good job, Ekta! Now you see how powerful your thoughts are," I exclaimed happily. "You know how I'm always telling you to send the right messages to yourself? Well now you see what I mean. Your brain needs to send the right information. If you think about dropping the egg, some part of you is sending the wrong message to your fingers."

Benjamin interrupted. "Oh Mom, is this going to be one of your epics on confidence?"

"I don't know. Should it be?"

"Come on, Ekta," he said. "Let's not get her going." And they headed off to find the cats while I started dinner: curried chicken salad, thrown together from leftovers. No recipe!

So, dear one, there's more I'd like to chat about but it will have to wait. Tomorrow is supposed to be stormy so I'll likely write to you again, or at least send some pages from my journal. I just want you to know how much our writing has healed inside me. This correspondence has been a lifeline. And because it's the anniversary of when we began I wanted to thank you again.

I'm sending much, much love and many wishes for all that's sweet about summer.

Journal: Last Friday of June

I'm sitting on the deck this hot and hazy last Friday of June. We are supposed to be having severe thunderstorms all day, so every moment of sunshine is a gift, delicious as a forbidden cookie. Given the forecast, I intended to spend most of the morning at the computer, but the sweet rosy scent on the breeze at my window lured me outdoors.

My roses are impossibly beautiful this year, the entire eight-foot shrub heavily laden with delicate white blossoms. Each one is perfect, because the Japanese beetles are late in arriving this summer. So here I will write, with the rose fragrance wrapped all around me and sweet alyssum too, from the planters on the deck. Pink peonies and peach poppies have opened in the pond garden. Further beyond, against the hazy green backdrop of the meadow, a few mostly lavender lupine still stand smartly amid pungent white valerian, the plant used for sleeping medicine. Its delicate blossoms float high above their tall stems like a hundred fairies on lacy butterfly wings.

I know the storm is coming. The wind tousles Bravo's mane and sends ripples lapping at the rock where three turtles bask in the shallow end of the pond. But the breeze is not strong enough to blow in a storm, not yet, so I'll wallow a while in this stolen peaceful moment.

There are things I should be doing, but I don't want to abandon this summer day for errands. I need to mail a birthday gift to Grandpa, pick up circus tickets, and make an appointment for Ekta's hepatitis shot (she always gets her shots the day the circus comes to town). Our animals are due for shots too: rabies for Brandy, West Nile booster for Bravo, and something-or-another for the kitties.

I also should make an appointment for Benjamin to have a haircut. And perhaps I'll make one for myself too, so she can fix my September 11 trim. I don't go to the beauty salon very often. The only other time last year was in April, when I was visiting the tanning machine there in preparation for our trip to Punta Cana. I laugh out loud now when I remember that day.

That was back when I had to lay out my clothes in the right order so I could dress properly without much thought. Somehow my bra had fallen out of my neatly-ordered pile on the chair. I didn't notice it until the end of my dressing ritual, at which point I simply hitched it around my waist. I was in a hurry, lots on my mind, and I zipped out the door. As I passed through the beauty shop, a woman with hair poking through the holes of a plastic cap regarded me searchingly, looking at my face longer than was necessary for a perfunctory greeting. I assumed she was admiring the golden freckled tan I'd developed thanks to the cooker in the closet. It wasn't until I was in my car, pulling the seatbelt across my lap, that I noticed the misplaced bra. Not sure how it had gotten there, but knowing it belonged someplace else, I unhitched it and pushed it under the car seat.

I'm pleased those things don't happen much anymore. Yet I also realize it wouldn't trouble me a whole lot now if they did. Yesterday as I was driving home alone after dropping the children off at their camp programs, I was having a sort of chicken-or-egg conversation in my head. I was wondering if the reason I'm feeling happier and more relaxed about myself these days is because I'm better—meaning that I'm starting to somewhat resemble who I used to be: capable, independent, and gaining in confidence. Or am I actually happier and more relaxed because I've finally arrived at a place where who I used to be doesn't matter much any more.

Not that the answer to that question (if there is one answer) has any heuristic value. But it's perhaps useful to remember how critical attitude is in shaping events. Of course events also shape attitude, so here we are—back to the chicken and the egg. It is true though that events are often beyond my realm of efficacy, whereas attitude is always something I can choose to craft in my own heart.

I don't mind so much the dumb things I say or do now, probably because they no longer represent a loss of self. Of course, I use a lot of strategies effectively to function now, and that certainly makes things better. But something else has changed too: At one time each mishap was not only embarrassing, inconvenient, or dangerous—it was also an arrow piercing the lost self I was grieving. The arrows are gone now. Maybe that's why things seem better. Or perhaps it's the target that's gone—a self cracked wide open and vulnerable, like a lobster that's shed its shell and hasn't yet grown a new one.

The weekend before Maine, Michael and I were camping with Ekta's scouts (in miserable rain and forty-one degrees) at Buck Lake, where Vermont's Fish and Wildlife Department conducts a conservation camp. We went hiking and canoeing, learned archery, found our way with a compass, created survivor fishing rods out of soda cans and string, and built bluebird houses. That fully packed twenty-four hours was more than I could handle—but I knew it might be, and that's why Michael came along. We arrived home drenched and exhausted at five-thirty in the evening. Ten minutes later I was in bed and did not wake up until nine the next morning.

Michael and Ekta hung the new bluebird house on the far side of the weeping willow, down next to the tamaracks, whose cute rosebud-shaped pinecones look like buttons on a fancy sweater. Now we have bluebirds!

I first saw them the morning after we returned from Maine, when I was moving the better Big Boy tomato plants out of the bathtub, where they'd been kenneled for safekeeping while we were away. Our weather has not been too tomato-friendly yet this summer, so we thought they were safer in the bathtub than the garden. Anyway, I was looking out the window while my bath was filling—waiting to pour some luxurious bath oil, a gift from my sister Marsie, into the steamy tub—and I saw those unmistakable cobalt wings. One bird was perched atop the bluebird house. Then I noticed a second one on the post that holds the badminton net in place.

I went downstairs to tell Ekta. She was listening to Dan Fogelberg's song "Longer Than," which I used to sing as her lullaby—only I improvised on the lyrics a bit. The first time she heard his recording, she told me he didn't know the words and suggested that I write them out for him. Now I found her standing at the bay window, barefoot in red flannel boxers. Shirtless, her young breasts peaked like stiff chocolate meringue, her black hair wild. She had not heard me come into the room; she and Dan F. were singing too loudly.

I watched her remove the lids from her watercolor paint jars. Methodically, she lined them up next to the board where her painting paper was already taped into place. Then she picked up her brush and looked a long while toward the misty meadow. I wondered what she was thinking, what she would create out of this wet gray-green morning. Outside, sitting on my chaise lounge, Shadow kitty peered in through the window and watched Ekta's brush sweep the first stroke of color across her paper. Silently, I returned to my bath.

I picked up my novel, the one Michael bought at the beach when he and Benjin went for lobster rolls and passed a newspaper shop with paperbacks. This is my second novel this year. Short chapters, large print, not too many characters, a predictable sequence that moves forward chronologically, simple plot. I can handle it, especially if I read large chunks at a time. I don't process all of it, just the essential parts. *Nora Nora* is about a twelve year-old girl amidst the angst of adolescence and racial integration in small-town Georgia 1961. A good book for me to be reading now.

One errand I definitely want to do today is to stop in town and speak with the librarian. Perhaps there's some young adult literature I could read with Ekta to help with that "too awful to talk about" question. A journal or diary maybe, written by a young girl. A girl like herself—spirited, brave, and wise. One who wants to believe in the goodness of people.

What a therapeutic process writing is, for both the writer and the reader. I am grateful for people brave enough to tell their stories. Driving past the vacated school buildings the other day, it struck me how vital literacy is, and how ludicrous the reading tutor/para-educator salary is. I checked into that as part of my vocational rehab process, considering that I might like to help children learn to read and write, children with brains that work a little differently. If I were a reading tutor, the school would pay me five dollars per hour. If I provide one hour of psychotherapy, the insurance company pays me eighty-five dollars. Given the disproportionate number of learning-disabled people in prison populations and mental health settings, I wonder why we don't place a higher premium on literacy.

When I came down from my bath there was a rainbow in the window: Ekta had propped her painting up to dry. I noticed a splotch in the purple band. Usually she's such a perfectionist about her painting that I expected this could mean the onset of a terrible day.

"I got a big air bubble in the purple," she said matter-of-factly.

"Oh dear, that's too bad." I paused, trying to gauge her reaction, then added, "Maybe you can wait until it dries and then repair it."

But she wasn't upset at all. "No. Just look at this color, Mom. I couldn't blend that same purple again in a million years."

"Yeah, it really is a wonderful shade of purple, isn't it?"

"So is this green. It took me forever to make this color. It's just right, isn't it?"

And it was. Just like the fresh wet green outside. "Yes," I told her, "your rainbow is beautiful. All the colors are exquisite."

"You know, I don't really mind about that air bubble," she said. "Real rainbows probably have lots of air bubbles."

I expect they do.

Journal: July 9, 2002

Tuesday evening, seven-thirty p.m., and still sunny on our side of the meadow. The hill behind isn't tall enough to cast a shadow this far as the sun sinks slowly into its leafy canopy. Beyond our meadow the wetlands are still sunny too. Michael and Ekta are out there in the old silvery canoe, their orange and yellow life vests bright in this evening light. They are heading off to check on the beavers, who seem to be engineering a flood across the road.

A tree frog who lives in the rain spout above our hammock has begun his serenade to the frog in the birch tree. They sing to one another every night that isn't rainy. The clematis vines have finally made it to the top of the deck railing, and how lovely they are. After the big storm a few weeks ago I was afraid they were too broken to blossom, but the kids helped me tie them up and all are blooming brilliantly now. We tied the white roses back up too, after the storm laid most of the branches flat on the lawn.

That same storm sent a tree tumbling onto one of the tents at the Girl Scout camp-out. Fortunately, the girls had already evacuated and were safe in the Elmore fire station. When I told Benjamin about it the next day, he said that Ekta must have loved sleeping in the firefighters' loft. "Remember how she always dreamed of being a firefighter?" he asked.

I do remember that, but I told him that this actually was pretty hard for her. "She's kind of fragile, dainty, and doesn't like getting bumped and bruised," I said. "The loft was crowded and the storm was scary."

"Ekta's not dainty," he replied. "She's actually really tough. She just doesn't know it yet, because she lacks confidence." He's right, of course, and I was struck by his insight.

I used to think that a person became confident by discovering all her capabilities and figuring out there was very little terrain where she could not endeavor to be successful. Self-confidence was the crowning glory for those few who were lucky enough to be good at most things. That made sense to me before my injury, but it doesn't any more. I have many limitations now, but I have managed to find my confidence again. Rather than relying upon a critical quotient of capabilities, it seems to grow more from self-awareness and acceptance.

I am confident now because I know what I can do well and what I can't. I accept my limitations, use my strategies, and ask for help when I need it. I remember one of my earliest appointments with Dr. Musiek, when he was explaining that the key for both Benjamin and me would be to build on our strengths and plan to accommodate our limitations. Being successful was a matter of orchestrating capabilities and limitations. He told me, "You'd be surprised to discover the many limitations of highly visible, effective people. They just structure situations so they can be at their best."

I didn't get it at that time but I do now: Confidence doesn't come from being good at everything. In fact, the only thing you have to be good at is knowing and accepting yourself. And, as my thirteen year-old son aptly put it, when you find your confidence you discover how tough you really are.

17

The Broken Jar

Journal: July 11, 2002

The white roses are still blooming and the yellow primrose too. And Buttercup seems to be a broody hen. We'll have
to decide whether to give her some eggs that will hatch or let
her sit on nothing until she gives up. When Lyndall returns
from ski camp in the Alps, we could ask her for fertile eggs.

I remember the day Michael and I collected our first
baby chicks from Lyndall. It was in the springtime, nearly
eight months after my accident. We were standing in her
front hall, the box full of peeping chickens at our feet. And
she suddenly realized she had mixed up her schedule and
almost forgotten to meet her children on time. As she was
rushing out the door she said, "See, it must be comforting
for you to know you're not the only one with that problem.
Lots of people have memory problems and get mixed up
about what they're supposed to be doing." I knew she was
trying to offer comfort and reassurance, as she has done so
often throughout my recovery. But that day her words left

me feeling agitated. As I carried our wee chicks to the car, I wondered why.

If I had been able to articulate feelings into thoughts and words at the time, I might have tried to explain. I might have asked her, "If you had suffered a skiing injury while you were on the pro tour and now could only snowplow your way down a mountain, would it help to be reminded that a lot of people can't even snowplow?" But that type of reasoning was beyond my capability in those days, so I sat quietly with the chirping chicks on my lap as Michael drove us home.

Just a couple weeks ago, I found an envelope on the porch swing. Lyndall had been by while I was out and left an article she'd cut from the newspaper about how brain injuries change people's lives. As I read the interviews and commentary several times over, the words crystallized much of my own wondering from these past three years. The article described a patient whose brain scans were normal but who had debilitating ailments. And it noted that people often are permanently altered by their injuries.

I realized that what is initially most troubling for brain injury patients is their diminished ability to function. "Not doing the things I used to do" translates pretty quickly into "not being the person I used to be." It is that perceived loss of self that lingers and can become so devastating. The article quoted a doctor who said that people whose lives are changed by brain injury actually have to grieve for themselves.

Yes, that's right, I thought. And my children and husband grieve too. Until one day we discover we are no longer grieving.

Christin, dear one,

I have just finished reading your *Altar Music*. Breathtakingly beautiful!! Oh my, how tenderly you handle the most aching things. I am glad now that I didn't continue the story with Michael reading to me but waited until I could do it myself, with only a few notes to keep track of the people and story. Poetry on every page, and the stunning truths revealed so delicately. I would have missed all of that. And I could have been stuck in the pain of it, all that loss, at a time when I might not have been able to go beyond the tragedy. Now I can savor it. And there is so much of you in the story, lovely Christin, so much beauty and wisdom. I treasure every word, every ordinary thing made profoundly elegant and significant because of your exquisite voice and knowing heart.

One of my most healing bits of wisdom was right there on the pages of *Altar Music,* at the end. You had already written it to me long ago in an e-mail, but it was wonderful to hear Sister Mary tell Elise, "Remember, there's no hurry. You have your whole life." Sister Mary sounds so like you, Christin. I love her music notebooks. And the part when Elise remembered Sister's words: "When grief is overwhelming you keep your fingers on the keys closest to your body." "And keep playing. Play through it to the end," Sister Mary added. "A time will come when you will discover within yourself everything you imagined that you lost."

You can imagine how I might be struck by the power of those words, revealing something that now finally I know to be true. Thank you for your precious words, words that are like music.

I'm really happy to hear that you're doing well with your exercising. Studies seem to indicate that aerobic fitness is great for brain health and functioning. Brains like oxygen and good food too. Brain tissue makes up only two percent of total body weight but uses one-third of the day's calories and a quarter of the oxygen. So what we feed ourselves is really important. Blueberries and blackberries are good for the brain, I seem to remember, and lots of vitamin C. In any event, I wanted to send you this quick note about *Altar Music*, now that I've been able to read it. I hope you and the bears are keeping happy company on your morning walks.

My love is with you always.

Journal: July 2002

Recently I've been wondering what personality is: where does our essence reside? Surely it can't be limited to the neurons and chemicals of the brain—or can it? After my injury, my mother commented frequently how fortunate we were that I was not plagued with the disinhibitions and drastic personality changes that often accompany brain injury. I'm also lucky to be one of the few brain-injured (less than twenty-five percent) whose marriages don't rip apart along with their torn neural pathways. Understanding how easily that could happen, I am forever grateful to be blessed with a patient and forgiving family.

One day Michael and I had a particularly bad argument. He said he was tired of always being the one to make all the adjustments, constantly accommodating to my diminished abilities. "I'm human, and sometimes I just don't like it," he said.

"Listen, you're not the only one making adjustments here," I told him. "My whole life is an adjustment."

I was shoveling manure down at the barn later, when he returned from the grocery store with a bouquet. He said the flowers were scraggly, but this one was the best of the bunch.

"I know this is hard," I said. "And I don't expect you to be a saint. Most of the time you are a saint, but I just want you to know I don't expect it."

Journal: July 2002

For a year now, Kwan Yin has been in my garden and my heart, working her special magic. She sits amidst a bed of Roman wormwood, a lacy silver-green carpet quite suitable for a goddess. Kwan Yin is her Chinese name, the one that was printed neatly on her tag when I picked her up from the nursery last summer. When I arrived home there was nobody around to help me unload her, so I parked on the lawn above the garden and rolled her down the hill. That's not a particularly graceful entrance for a goddess, but it doesn't seem to have compromised her generous spirit.

In India she is called Tara, Mother of All the Buddhas, Goddess of Compassion. After the Lord and Bodhisattva of Compassion himself had given up in despair, it was she who arose out of his tears and vowed to help. Devotees will tell you that she is the most willing goddess—the one who will rush to your aid as soon as you think of her, even if you never believed in her before.

Yesterday I planted white alyssum and pink dianthus at her feet, just in front of the mossy rock wall. After carrying several buckets of water from the pond to the garden I sat to rest on one of the warm gray stones and remembered the story from India about a village boy who brought water to the wealthy man.

Every day he walked several miles from the village to the river and back again, carrying water in two clay jars, one in his left hand and one in his right. The man paid for the water that was delivered—one full jar and one half full, for the jar in one hand was cracked and its water leaked out along the roadside. Over the long months, the boy made many trips carrying water.

One day he sat to rest before returning to the river, and a spirit in the cracked jar spoke to him. "I am sorry, Master, that you have to work harder because of me. If I were perfect like your other jar, you would not need to take so many trips. And you could collect more money, too. I am sorry that because of me your life is made miserable."

The boy was surprised to hear such words. He did not think his life was miserable. He replied to the spirit, "Because of you, I am very lucky. A broken jar makes my life beautiful. Come, let me show you."

Together they walked back to the river. One side of the path was bare and dusty. But along the other side, where water had trickled down from the broken jar, the way was strewn with wildflowers.

It's been three summers now since Nanny sent me a generous birthday check to mark the threshold of my forties. What a threshold it was! How different life might have been if I'd used the money to buy myself a garden rocker instead of a riding helmet—a decision that enrolled me in a series of lessons far greater than any I could have imagined.

Throughout my recovery from this brain injury there have been many unexpected gifts—not just for me, but for Michael and the children too. Time and again we experienced the blessing of unanswered prayers, moments of glad grace throughout this mending journey.

Kwan Yin's presence in my garden reminds me that despair can be transformed. Even though things turned out differently than I might have hoped three years ago, truly now I see how a broken jar makes life beautiful.

Journal: July 2002

This morning I awoke to the sound of a fire-breathing dragon outside my bedroom window. I've never actually heard a dragon, but I imagine it would sound quite like the bellows that hurl fire up inside a hot air balloon. Just before seven this morning, a whole fleet of them sailed overhead. One thing I love about our meadow is its suitability for balloon landings.

This was certainly an improvement over yesterday morning, which began when Ekta, waking from a nightmare, crawled into the last few inches of available space in our bed.

"What time is it?" Michael asked her.

"I don't know," she said.

"Look at the clock."

"It says SOS."

"That's 5:05, Ekta. It's too early to wake up."

"But I had a really scary dream," she protested. "I don't want to go back to bed. Not unless you come with me."

The sounds of dragon breath had not yet disturbed her sleep this morning and I debated whether to wake her. But the balloons were simply too beautiful to miss—thirteen of them all coming our way. So I drew her curtains and roused her out of bed. Together we went outside, warm jackets covering our nightgowns.

The last two balloons floated into our neighborhood and settled, one by the organic farm down the road and one right next to us, in Peter and Sherry's driveway. As tradition dictates, the pilot produced a bottle of champagne for the landowners. That ritual offering commenced back in the earliest days of ballooning, when angry farmers arrived with pitchforks to defend against what they believed really might be flying dragons. Just yesterday, a farmer up in Mud City called the police when an errant balloon landed in his pasture. Evidently this had happened previously, and his cows were so disturbed by the ordeal they produced no milk. Even champagne failed to appease them.

The balloon travelers who visited here this morning told us that story and many others as we shared mimosas made of champagne and orange juice. Sherry rode up a distance once the balloon was tethered to the car. So did Michael, with Benjamin and Ekta. But I remained earthbound, sitting on the porch with Peter, who was recovering from surgery after having a heart attack on a flight from London's Heathrow Airport. He told me that he had felt just awful and knew something was not right. "I went into the bathroom," he said, "and when I looked in the mirror, I didn't recognize myself."

Peter would not describe himself as a particularly religious person. "I've always tried to live pretty close to the Ten Commandments. But the mountain is my church. So that day on the plane when I looked into the mirror, I just said 'OK, big fella, if you're going to pull the plug, could you please just let me cross over into Vermont?'"

I listened, sitting there in my nightclothes, sipping orange juice on his sunny terrace. "And you know," Peter continued, "something really happened then. He let me come home to these mountains." We were both admiring the Worcester range, so blue this morning, and hazy. "When I woke up after my operation I realized, 'I'm alive!'

And nothing else mattered. All those things I was so worried about, I don't care about them at all. Not in the way that I used to, like they were a heavy weight on my shoulders, a real burden."

I replied, "It's pretty unbelievable, isn't it, when something like that happens, how everything else simply fades away. Those things that we thought mattered very greatly—they all fade away. And you're just so happy to be here, sitting here right now in this amazing life."

I don't ever want to forget that: *Precious little matters greatly.* Perhaps I can etch it into my memory, along with the splendid sight of that huge fiery balloon floating down out of our hazy summer sky.

Journal: July 25, 2002

Our bluebird pair is busy this morning—back and forth, back and forth, feeding their babies. I heard them for the first time yesterday when I was in the meadow with Bravo, that unmistakable cry of hungry birds as the mother flies in with food. I'm elated; these are the first bluebirds ever to hatch out in one of our boxes.

I've started swimming again. Last night at the pool, while the children had their lesson, I did laps for the entire half hour and was pleased to be capable of that much. The practice of breathing on both sides gives me a new, more balanced rhythm; I like the feeling. As my arm muscles began to tire, I remembered my older sister's warning about "wiggling flesh."

Every summer when we get together, Marsie clues me in on what to expect in the aging process. Since she's exactly one year older and we have mostly similar bodies, she sets a good example of what I'll look like soon enough. "Wrinkles above your kneecaps," she told me, "and arm muscles that wiggle when you put on blush. That's really the worst—to be looking at your face in the mirror and see all this stuff shaking on your arm." Then she added reassuringly, "Of course that won't be a problem for you, because you don't wear make-up. So at least you won't see it jiggling every day."

Remembering that little conversation while swimming laps made me smile. I pulled harder through the water and kicked a little faster too. I don't know if exercise can truly help ward off wrinkles and jiggles, but it does keep a brain healthy.

The last day that my sisters and I were together at my parents', Bobba decided to review his burial and funeral plans with us. I'm not entirely sure what prompted him. Perhaps it was his granddaughters' harrowing adventure: river tubing while lightning struck all around. The sky had been clear blue when the girls posed for photos before setting out. But the storm blew in swiftly, just after the current had carried them out of sight. Within minutes, thunder and lightning were cracking all around us, and there was nothing to do but pray.

As things turned out, the girls fared well—even Ekta, who is terrified of lightning. At the first huge crack, which Jenna said was right beside them, they scrambled up the rocky, root-tangled bank. Bethany thought they might be able to reach the road through the cornfield. But Jenna remembered stories about kids getting lost in high cornfields. So they made their way along the edge of the field and eventually we met up, drenched and freezing.

Hours later, when we all were happily sipping malts at the café, Bobba told us he had changed his mind about being buried at the military cemetery in Pennsylvania and had purchased a plot in town. He said he wants to be cremated, which troubled Barli immensely. She told Marsie and me later that it's gruesome—so irreverent, a heap of bodies all burned up together, and you don't get your own ashes.

"You can pay extra to be cremated alone," Marsie said.

I wondered what the point of that would be. You don't get to keep your own ashes anyway. Besides, what do you need them for? It's all a question of relinquishment, really. The question of what to do with the precious things in life. We let go a little bit at a time. And sometimes we have to let go of a lot, all at once.

Barli told us she can't bear the thought of Bobba being cremated. I said, "Maybe he can't bear the thought of being chewed up by bugs."

"No, that's not it," Marsie said. "He told us it costs too much; that's why he doesn't want a coffin and burial. It's expensive to prepare a body." Barli said she's going to work on getting him to change his mind about this cremation idea.

I said I'd work on the Mass, since we should probably write a letter to get it set up. They looked at me curiously. "This isn't like a wedding, you know, not something you set a date for," Marsie said. Then I realized how stupidly my brain was putting the information together. It's just the way I work now. I have my calendar ready in every conversation, organizing details so they don't disappear before I grasp them. Usually it's a good strategy.

"He's only seventy-five," I said aloud to myself, "and very healthy. We don't need to make advance reservations for a funeral High Mass."

I kissed my sisters goodbye and headed up the gulch toward Moss Glen Falls. I started thinking about my own funeral or memorial and where I would be buried, cremated or not. I was surprised at how matter-of-factly I seemed to be contemplating the whole affair. I guess that's another thing that comes with age. Or perhaps it comes with brain injury: acceptance of mortality and daily practice in relinquishment.

Along with her counsel about wrinkles and jiggly flesh, Marsie also brought me up to date on the current trends in lingerie (cellophane bra straps that are invisible for summer fashions) and backyard cuisine (whole fryers barbecued on a full can of beer—Benjin calls it "Beer-up-the-Butt Chicken"). And she patiently set up my checking account on the computer, slowly going over every detail numerous times while I took notes. I think I can actually do it now, and that will mean Michael no longer has to balance the account, as he has been doing since my accident. That's the only piece of our financial affairs that I have yet to reclaim, so this is a milestone indeed.

Last week I called several hospitals in the Boston area trying to find the Harvard affiliate where they developed the Memory 101 course for brain-injured, stroke, and Alzheimer's patients. I was hoping to collect some practical advice and suggestions to share with others who have cognitive deficits like mine. I never found what I was looking for, so I thought perhaps I could write about the systems I know, my own strategies. That's when Marsie volunteered to be a guinea pig and follow my directions for setting up her own file box and basket. She was pretty excited, and so was Jenna. "This is going to be a good thing, Mom. Maybe the counter by our phone will even be neat now."

That's how I feel about my brain, too. What used to be a jumbled mess is now becoming relatively neat. It's as though an executive director has been recruited from the surrounding circuitry; someone who knows how to handle the flow of information is now sitting at the desk. I think perhaps the process of using my compensatory strategies has actually helped to recruit and rewire neurons for the job. I don't know that for sure; I just wonder if it might be true. Empirical evidence does indicate that neurogenesis occurs across the life span. Even the brain tissue of end-stage cancer patients is engaged in creating new neurons.

E-MAIL: TO CHRISTIN
DATE: AUGUST 14, 2002

Christin, dear friend,

Your last e-mail about the fires was alarming; you've been in my heart and prayers every moment. Fortunately, there are no Oregon fires in the national headlines, thank God! I'm hoping that means your forests are not ablaze like they were last summer. You wrote about being terrified of fire and now here you are, living in a "red zone," thinking about what to put in your car so you'll be ready to leave in a hurry if the flames reach the gulch and catch wind. Perhaps we are drawn to face our fears.

As I read through your description of packing a steamer trunk, I got to wondering. If our house were burning, what would I want to save? And my immediate response was: *As long as I have my children, I could live without the rest.* (In my scenario, Michael was already safe at work).

The absolute clarity of my answer surprised me a little. I used to think about that "what would you save in a fire" question from a variety of perspectives, most recently as a closet-cleaning exercise. My response always used to be more complex. This time it was refreshingly simple, and I know it's true.

But as I read through your letter again I wondered—when I am your age how will I answer that question? My children will be grown and gone from here. My parents may be gone. And there may still be treasures of my beloveds neatly tucked away in my home. If fire lit the sky in the hills around this house, I probably would be up late packing a steamer trunk, just like you.

Interesting, isn't it, what we cling to at different stages of life? I like what you said about how each object awakens something in your life, each is a key to who you are. "These beloved things are symbols; even more than symbols, they are sacraments of the presence of those we love."

"It's a question of relinquishment," you also wrote, "a foretaste of death. All of life is so beautiful, and so fragile. That's the lesson of it." It truly is, isn't it?

Well, dear one, I do hope you are well, safe from the fires and impossible questions.

18

Shiny Shoes

E-MAIL: TO CHRISTIN
DATE: AUGUST 21, 2002

Good morning lovely Christin,

I'm so happy to wake this morning with nothing on the calendar and nobody at home (the children went camping with a friend last night), so I have a few minutes to talk with you.

We're on our final stretch of summer vacation. Then it's off to sixth grade and eighth grade. And back to book-writing for me. After a huge nightmare with the scanner and scanning software, I had to take a break. Benjamin was an amazing help; I never could have done it without him. But I did develop a crazy thing in my wrist—mouse tendonitis, a ridiculous nuisance. I said to Michael, "Maybe this is a sign. The scanner doesn't work and neither does my hand."

He said, "You and your 'signs.' The only thing this means is that it's going to be harder than you thought. So take a rest and then get back to work."

A few days later I was wondering about vaccinating Bravo. When I went online to look up information on West Nile Virus, I stumbled upon the very article about Memory 101 (the Harvard course on brains and memory) that I lost a few weeks ago and had been unable to locate again. Well that was pretty weird, to have it just pop up in front of me when I thought I was seeking out West Nile Virus. "Maybe that's a sign," I said. Michael laughed.

Maybe I'm supposed to keep working at the book. I'll start again Monday, first day of school.

We decided to forego our end of summer trip this year and put the money toward the purchase of a tiny filly. "Velvet Flirtation" is her name. Ekta tells me she's just perfect, and I could see that the moment they met. We had driven up to the horse farm simply to visit the new babies. "Flirt" was in the field with her mother and when Ekta went through the gate, Flirt came right over. They spent the hour together, smelling and nuzzling each other and frolicking in the paddock. Each time I said we had to go, Ekta headed reluctantly to the gate, but tiny Flirt came right along as if to say, "Don't go. Please. Not yet." We returned yesterday and brought the deposit check—all of Ekta's bank account and more.

Our pond has been a pure luxury this summer. On the surface the temperature feels like bath water, but the cold springs below remind me that I'm in a pond. So does the grassy weed growing in the shallow by the rocks. Mermaid hair, I call it. But it makes a nice home for leeches, the ones that arrive from faraway places on the feet of migrating geese. So we have to pull the mermaid hair out by its roots.

I never used to know what the pond looked like below its cloud-reflecting surface, because I always closed my eyes underwater. But one day I decided to swim laps here instead of at the health club. So I put on my cap and goggles, mostly out of habit. I set off swimming with my eyes open and realized for the first time how truly beautiful pond water is. Murky green but infused with light rays. Quite spectacular, especially in the late afternoon when the sun is low in the sky and the light slants in from behind the garden where Kwan Yin sits. With each stroke, hundreds of light-filled bubbles form around my fingers. The entire experience is ecstatic and meditative. Every third stroke I turn my head for air. On one side, I breathe in the hazy blue mountain ridges; the next breath takes in the flowers from my garden. Always, my lungs empty into the pond, breath gradually bubbling into the sunlit silence of the water.

Yesterday Benjamin said he thought he would start writing in the blank book that Grandma Jeanne gave him a couple years ago. That's a huge milestone for him, as you know his challenge with writing. To actually want to write something that was not absolutely necessary and required for school has been unheard of before now. Although I should mention that this summer a friend of mine who is a speech and language therapist wrote to ask if Benjamin might be an e-mail writing pal for one of her students, eleven year-old Ryan, who is dealing with many of the same challenges Benjamin had to overcome.

Benjamin's first response was, "I'm not very good at that kind of thing."

I said, "You *are* good at that kind of thing, a lot better than you think. And you understand how hard it can be, so you're a lot smarter than most people. I'm sure that's why she asked you. But you can think about it and let me know later. It's nothing you have to do. Lori just wanted to ask, but she'll find somebody else if you don't want to."

The next day he told me that he had decided to write to Ryan. At least to try, but he said again that he wasn't sure if he could do it very well. As it turned out, Ryan was the one who decided not to write. Lori e-mailed to tell us that it was just too hard for him to let anybody see his writing now, because he thinks it's not good enough. So the correspondence never happened.

But Benjamin said, "That's OK if he doesn't write to me. I still want to send him a letter and tell him that nobody could possibly be as bad at writing as I used to be. So he doesn't need to be embarrassed about it. And he probably thinks he's the only one who can't do it. I want to write to him just so he knows he's not alone, he's not the only one. And I can tell him everything turns out OK if you just keep working at it. He probably doesn't know that either."

So Benjamin began his journal last night. He had asked earlier what kind of things to write about in a journal. He's read a lot of mine these past few months as he has helped me scan and convert my entries into chapters, but he wasn't sure what exactly he should write about. I told him you can write anything in a journal. Whatever is on your mind, things that you might not be ready to say to anybody else, you can say in your journal. And you can write about what happens in your life; sometimes writing helps you figure out the hard stuff. When I went to bed his light was still on and he was writing away.

Well, dearest Christin, send me word of your summer days and heart's pondering when you have a chance. In the meantime, know how greatly I love you. Please be well.

I was in the shower yesterday morning getting ready for church, and a thought came to me the way thoughts often do there—as if they just fall out of the water droplets. I realized that these past several months spent with my book have been great training for my brain. In somewhat the same way that going through piles of photographs in the first half year after the accident helped me get oriented again, I think that the organization of the manuscript chronologically has helped me grasp the whole picture. The mental gymnastics involved in the task have been grueling, but that great effort may have been the point and purpose.

Thinking this, I started laughing, because it dawned on me once again, for the hundredth time in my life, how process really is the thing that matters. *Trust the process.* I've said that so often to clients. I really do believe that when you hit whitewater, the best course is through it. You've got to stay in the canoe and keep paddling. Don't jump out! Or, like you said in *Altar Music,* keep your fingers on the keys closest to your body and keep playing.

With the manuscript almost completed now, I understand a lot more about the healing journey than I ever would have if I'd abandoned the process. I think my brain has developed a few more channels and I have more "storage files" as a result of the organizing and sequencing challenges, too. Certainly, it took a fair bit of "new learning" to get the text out of my journals and binders full of paper and to load everything onto my computer.

Many times I nearly stopped, because it seemed that any book assembled from this heap of notes would be really dull and I was having so much trouble just putting them in order.

But I kept returning to the work because I thought if it could help even one person through a hard spot in life, then it would be worth doing. Yesterday in the shower, I was laughing because that one person turns out to be me! And once again I had to acknowledge that funny thing about humans: how often, when we set out to help others, what we're really doing is helping ourselves.

I dressed and took the children to church alone because Michael had a baby to deliver. In her sermon, Maggie told us about the labyrinth she visited this summer in an old churchyard in Concord, Massachusetts. She said that labyrinths are unicursive, meaning they are made from only one line, so it's impossible to get lost if you just keep on going. That's what ancient wisdom teaches. Keep on walking (or paddling the canoe, playing the music, writing, or working at recovery). Whatever it is, just keep on, and eventually you'll find your way.

Remember I asked you once how I would know when to end my story? I could go on writing until I'm ninety, but at what point in time do I say, "I'm recovered. The end." Vocational Rehab is the last piece of formal recovery work. My counselor says that stage ends when I start making money; her job is over when I get a paycheck. In that sense, my recovery hasn't ended. But most brain injury literature says that nobody ever fully recovers from TBI.

I like your answer better. You told me, "The symbol of completion could be just about anything. A paycheck is one symbol, because in our culture gainful employment and money is something everyone understands. But what is it for *you*?" You gave the question back to me to answer for myself. You suggested that there would be a moment of closing a circle that has been open since the accident. "It can be very simple," you said. "You'll know it when it happens."

So I wanted to tell you, my ever-wise friend, that I think it happened—yesterday, in the shower.

Journal: September 2002

Barli's birthday is this month. I'm sending her a journal. That's not what I'd planned to buy when I stepped into the Haymaker gift shop last week. I was looking at a book with a pretty cover and inspirational verses when a woman came up to me and said, "You're PJ, aren't you?"

I looked up to see a woman I didn't know, and answered her question. "Yes, I'm PJ Long."

"This is perfect," she said. "I was trying to find you." She went on to explain that she knows a mother with four children who just moved here from New York City. Her husband died last year in the Twin Towers and she is trying to find a therapist for her children. This stranger in the gift shop told me that my name kept coming up, that I had a great reputation, and that she was happy to meet up with me like this because she knew I'd left my old office but didn't know where I'd gone.

I told her I'm not in practice anymore and I gave her the names of some therapists who might be able to help. Then she asked what I'm doing now. I told her I'm writing a book. "What's it about?" she asked. Sort of without thinking, I said that I guess it's about life—my slice of life. I didn't mention anything about my accident; it seemed irrelevant.

We talked for a few more minutes. Then she said she hoped those other therapists would be good. "You seem like such a real person," she told me. Under different circumstances, I would have thought that sounded odd. But the whole encounter was a bit surreal. As she left the shop I wondered whether she possibly could have known that now, finally, after three years of working at it, I actually do feel like a "real person" again.

Our conversation left me stunned, as I thought about those four children and their mother. I put down the book with the pretty cover and the inspirational verses and wandered over to the section with photos from a local photographer. Flipping through the photos was like a soothing balm. I stopped at one, a picture of a baby lamb with her mama, and knew it would be just right for my Barli. She has always wanted sheep. She has a spinning wheel and a "fiber group" of weavers and knitters, but no sheep. With four young children, there's no room for sheep.

One day she had called me in a funk. "This just isn't what I envisioned for my life. Not like there's anything so terrible about it, but it's just not how I pictured things when I dreamed about what my life would be." She continued on for a while and then stopped abruptly, saying, "Why am I telling you this? Surely you know about things not turning out the way you dreamed they would."

And I said to her, "Yes, I know a little about that. But honey, the real problem is trying to fit your new self into your old dreams: It doesn't work. You're not that person anymore, the one who first came up with that dream. Now you're a mother—a wonderful, wise, dedicated, and talented mother of four lovely, spirited children. You're much more than you used to be and your life is filled with more. You can't stuff all that into old dreams."

I asked the store clerk if she could mount the lamb photograph onto a blank book. It would be just right for my sister, for anybody really. Because we all need a place for new dreams, dreams that grow and change as life shapes and molds us the way it tends to do. When you get right down to it, we only pretend to know where we're headed. Truly we're all dreaming in the transit lounge, for none of us really know what life's labyrinth will hold.

Journal: September 2002

The songbirds are gone from the birch tree outside my bedroom window and just this week I've started hearing the ducks and geese, sounds that tell me autumn has arrived. My accident happened three years ago this week. It feels right that the end of my writing will coincide with that anniversary.

Yesterday Michael and I went walking through the old settlements around the Waterbury Reservoir. We followed the Hedgehog Road as it wound its way through two-hundred year-old farmsteads. Their mossy, rock-walled pastures were still neatly marked out along the wagon trail that passes stone-lined water wells, cellar holes, and a cemetery, now dwarfed by towering non-native arborvitae cedars.

We've been there before—years ago, before my accident —but yesterday we took in a lot more of the place, partly because there are markers at many of the sites now, so we knew what to look for in the overgrown thickets. And partly, I think, because we've slowed down enough to take it in: the moose tracks, berry-filled bear scat, and the stories that gravestones tell if you are paying attention.

As the Hedgehog Road intersected the Sawmill Road, we crossed paths with two riders on horseback. "A perfect day," I said to them. The scent of the horses lingered, mixed with the smell of wet autumn woods.

Further along the Sawmill Road, where day lilies and apple trees are the only hint that a farmhouse once stood there, Michael said, "Just so you know, most people wouldn't think this is a perfect day. That's not the customary thing to say when it's gray and raining." I got his point and started laughing. My comment to those riders was a little off.

I realized that I said the same thing to people last week when it was ninety-five and sweltering. I guess I *am* a little off, but to me the days do seem really quite good. I don't know if you need a brain injury to figure that out, but in my case it helped. Life is here, every moment, in its awesome, fragile, precious glory, and it waits for me. I don't have to go busily chasing after it. I am alive. I am loved. I have this moment now, and it really is enough.

When I was a little girl, I had a pair of dress-up shoes for special occasions. My sister Marsie and I each had a pair; we called them our "shiny shoes." They weren't kept in our closet, but were taken care of by a magical fox. Whenever we had occasion to need them, Mr. Fox appeared at our bedroom window and placed the shiny shoes on the windowsill. If we'd been tall enough to look out the window, we might have seen my dad crouched in the lantana bushes outside with the fox puppet on his hand. But we never did. We only saw the black patent leather shoes being delivered by Mr. Fox. And we knew that a special outing or important journey was about to take place.

During the first winter after my accident, I woke one night to the sound of a fox in the yard. I didn't get out of bed, but lay there listening to that haunting call which is quite like a human child's cry. It's very unusual to have a fox in our yard. In fact, during the ten years we've lived here, we've had only one other fox visit. That was shortly after Michael suddenly fell ill and took a midnight trip by ambulance to the hospital. It seemed to me then that the fox had appeared to reassure us things were going to be all right.

So that winter night, as I lay in bed listening to the fox beneath my window, I wondered if he had come with a message. I had a moment of mental clarity—which was unusual in those days—and I do remember the message. I saved it on a sticky note: "You haven't lost your husband or your children or your home. The only thing you've lost is yourself, and you can make a new self."

I never checked my window the next morning when I awoke. But perhaps if I had drawn the curtain back, I might have found a pair of black patent leather shoes waiting for me on the sill. Surely a remarkable journey lay ahead. I didn't know it then, but I would learn that losing oneself really means finding so much more in the end.

Notes and Acknowledgements

All of the journal entries and e-mails in this book were written during my recovery. As I assembled the manuscript, I tried to reconstruct an accurate chronology, and I made every effort to keep my original writing intact so that I could offer a realistic picture of my experience. A major exception is that the names and identifying characteristics of some individuals have been changed to assure their privacy.

I am immeasurably grateful for the many people whose presence in my life graced the pages of this book.

Thanks to my parents, Bob and Sue Long, for childhood lessons in patience and faith, and for believing in me, always. A special rose to my mother for her many kindnesses while helping to hold our household together after my accident.

Lilacs and apple blossoms to my sisters, Marsie Bryant and Barli Brown, and their families, and to my brother and his wife, Bo and Laurie Long, all of whom kept me in their hearts and prayers, helped in countless ways, and made me laugh.

Lupine meadows to my husband's parents, Bob and Jeanne Sampson and Nancy Sampson, for their unwavering support during trying times.

Golden oaks and mountain asters for Christin Lore Weber, sister of my soul, and my writing muse. Without her friendship, her beautiful spirit, wisdom, and words, this book would not exist.

Giant helianthus for the providers who cared for me during my recovery: Lakshmi Joshi-Boyle, SLP; Dr. Owen Drudge; Dr. Frank Musiek; all of the caring staff at Stowe Family Practice; and Carol Leech, my ever-enthusiastic, patient, and persistent vocational rehabilitation counselor.

Applause to the Brain Injury Association of Vermont, the Brain Injury Association of America, and TBI survivors everywhere—you are my inspiration! And special thanks to Jim Vyhnak and Lorraine Wargo for their help in launching this book.

Bouquets of wildflowers to the early readers of the manuscript whose feedback was invaluable: Mary Jo Braun, Mary Marlow, Sherry Strafford Rediger, and Jerri Andersen. A gardenia to Paul Bibbo for his encouragement.

Thanks to Benjamin Sampson, my in-house computer guru, for painstakingly converting the journal entries and e-mails into Word documents.

Butterfly iris for Sandra Scofield, who edited the manuscript with a writer's eye and an artist's heart.

Thanks to Mayapriya Long for lending her exquisite talent to the book's design. And to John Kremer and Linda Ramsdell for marketing and promotional help.

An arbor full of climbing roses to EquiLibrium Press and Susan Goland, who is truly an angel in disguise. Thanks for seeing the possibility in this book and working so hard to bring it to fruition; I can't imagine a more dedicated or savvy publisher.

Many friends and neighbors supported our family during my prolonged recovery: Reverend Maggie Rebmann and the members of the Unitarian Church of Montpelier; the community of the Green Mountain Waldorf School; and especially my children's teachers, Ursula Leonore and Alicia Benoit Clark, who was often "mom" to my Ekta when I couldn't be. A handful of daffodils to Ekta's kindred spirit, Jenna Zukswert, for her youthful optimism and encouragement. Immeasurable gratitude to Linda Hunter, Karen Sherman, Tracy Wrend, and the dedicated teachers at the Morrisville public schools for making a critical difference in our lives. Thanks to Lyndall Heyer, Scott Dorwart, Jeff Beattie, Mary Ellen Sudol, Margaret Haskins, Sarah Schlosser, and Leigh Lamphere for the rides, food, stories, garden help, and laughter. Bundles of pussy willows to Alicia, Jacob, Caleb, and Michael Clark, and to Helen Beattie, Matthew, Emma and Brendan Buckley, for perennial friendship.

I wish heaven's most glorious rainbow for Gretchen Siegfried, and her husband, Peter. Throughout her five-year journey with brain cancer, Gretchen was a radiant example of how "The sun shines not on us, but in us." That quote from John Muir was on the card Gretchen gave me shortly before her death.

And finally, snowy woods for my husband, Michael Sampson, whose love is my pillar of strength. And red and yellow tulips for my children, Benjamin and Ekta, because they help me plant the bulbs and every day remind me that life is our greatest teacher.

About the Author

Prior to her accident, PJ Long was a psychotherapist in private practice, an adjunct college professor, and a consultant. She holds dual masters degrees, one in interpersonal communication and a second in psychology and spirituality. Her undergraduate work included studies in England and Japan.

During her nearly twenty-year career in social services, PJ at various times worked at an orphanage in Bangladesh; counseled Saudi women leaving harem life; provided crisis intervention for troubled teens; led parenting groups; and consulted with corporations, hospitals, police, schools, and others.

PJ is married to Michael Sampson, a family practice physician, whose country doctoring includes house calls and delivering babies. They live in Vermont with their two children, a menagerie of barn animals, a pond full of frogs, and four gardens—none of which has ever produced a decent tomato.

Although this book grew out of PJ's experiences following her traumatic brain injury in 1999, a breast cancer diagnosis in 2003 affirmed her resolve to seek publication of the journals. Years of accompanying hundreds of clients through the broken places in their lives had helped prepare her for her own recovery. She is committed to sharing her journals so that she can pass on the gifts she has received to others who face arduous journeys.

PJ invites you to visit her website at *www.pjlong.com*. She also welcomes correspondence from readers. Please send your comments to: Gifts from the Broken Jar, P.O. Box 60, Morrisville, VT 05661 USA